WORLD WAR II

RAF AIRFIELDS in NORFOLK

AVIATION
HERITAGE TRAIL SERIES

WORLD WAR II
RAF AIRFIELDS in NORFOLK

Martin W. Bowman

Pen & Sword
AVIATION

First published in Great Britain in 2007 by
PEN & SWORD AVIATION
An imprint of
Pen & Sword Books Ltd
47 Church Street
Barnsley
South Yorkshire
S70 2AS

ISBN 978 1 84415 572 9

A CIP catalogue record for this book is
available from the British Library

Printed and bound in Great Britain
By CPI UK

Pen & Sword Books Ltd incorporates the Imprints of Pen & Sword Aviation,
Pen & Sword Maritime, Pen & Sword Military, Wharncliffe Local history,
Pen & Sword Select, Pen & Sword Military Classics and Leo Cooper.

For a complete list of Pen & Sword titles please contact
PEN & SWORD BOOKS LIMITED
47 Church Street, Barnsley, South Yorkshire, S70 2AS, England
E-mail: enquiries@pen-and-sword.co.uk
Website: www.pen-and-sword.co.uk

CONTENTS

INTRODUCTION

When in September 1939 Britain declared war on Germany the majority of airfields in Norfolk were occupied by RAF bomber squadrons. Bomber Command consisted of twenty-three home-based first-line squadrons and of these, six squadrons of Bristol Blenheim light bombers of 2 Group and six squadrons of Wellingtons of 3 Group (with two in reserve) were stationed in East Anglia. In Norfolk Wellingtons were first-line equipment for 37 Squadron at Feltwell and 38 and 115 Squadrons at Marham. Under the RAF Bomber Command 'Scatter' plan, the majority of bomber squadrons were immediately dispersed to satellite stations. The ten Bristol Blenheim squadrons in 2 Group were in five wings with 79 Wing at Watton (21 and 82 Squadrons) and 81 Wing at West Raynham (90 and 101 Squadrons). Four of the wings formed the 2nd echelon of the Advanced Air Striking Force while 70 Wing saw service in France supporting the British Expeditionary Force (BEF).

Heavy losses by day soon forced Bomber Command to continue the offensive at night, though losses continued to rise, and for the rest of the war Norfolk was in the front line with ever-increasing numbers of bomber, fighter-bomber and fighter squadrons stationed within its borders. And one must not forget the USAAF organizations which are covered in this series. Additionally, there is the famous 12 Group Fighter Command aerodrome at Coltishall and stations like Bircham Newton, Weybourne and Langham, which hosted Coastal Command units. Inland there were airfields occupied by 100 (Special Duties) Group (which are covered in a separate volume, although the periods in the Second World War when they saw operational use with other units, are covered here).

Kent has long been associated with the Battle of Britain and Lincolnshire is often referred to as 'Bomber County' but Norfolk is surely unique. This county emerged from six years of war to offer a rich diversity of Anglo-American airfields, whose proud legacy is only now threatening to disappear completely from the county's historical yet tranquil landscape. The tourist can combine visits to an abundance of disused and active airfields, country houses and museums with inland attractions, imaginative locations and broadland and coastal hideaways that have no equal.

Martin W. Bowman. Norwich, Norfolk

THE AIRFIELDS

ATTLEBRIDGE

Attlebridge airfield, which is in the parish of Weston Longville, was built during 1941–42 by Richard Costain Ltd for operation as a satellite airfield for Swanton Morley in RAF 2 Group, which operated light bombers, and the runways were 1,220, 1,120 and 1,080 yards long. In August 1941 Blenheim IV light bombers of 88 Squadron arrived from Swanton Morley and in September these aircraft were replaced by Boston IIIs. No.88 Squadron moved to Oulton in September 1942. The station was transferred to the USAAF although during March–August 1943 the airfield was used by 320 (Dutch) Squadron, RAF, flying B-25 Mitchells. No.320 had been formed in June 1940 from Dutch naval personnel and had moved from Methwold to Attlebridge to await re-equipment with the Mitchell II. The 'Flying Dutchmen' had been operating a motley collection of Ansons and Hudsons, mainly on convoy-protection and rescue duties from Northern Ireland, until they were transferred to 2 Group on 15 March.

In August they moved from Attlebridge to Lasham. Then for a time, some Typhoons and later war-weary US Navy PB4Y-1 Liberators used the airfield. Several small country roads were closed and the airfield was greatly

Corporal Jan Pronk and Piet den Haajer of 320 (Dutch) Squadron arming Mitchell II *Owe Jongens*. (*Jan P. Kloos*)

Attlebridge airfield is now lined with turkey-rearing sheds. (*Author*)

enlarged for heavy-bomber use. The main east–west runway was extended to 2,000 yards and the two others to 1,400 yards. The perimeter track was also extended and hardstandings increased to fifty pending the arrival of the USAAF. In July 1945 the station reverted to a satellite to 25 Maintenance Unit (MU) RAF Great Ashfield and was known as 94 Maintenance Sub-Unit. The airfield runways and Hockering Woods nearby were used to store bombs until August 1948. Up until December 1980 several of the wartime buildings remained, including a blister hangar and the control tower, while a number of smaller buildings were used by local farmers.

Attlebridge airfield was sold between 1959 and 1962, and Bernard Matthews Ltd, the largest integrated turkey company in Europe and probably the world, began using the runways for turkey-rearing operations and the buildings for administrative purposes.

BARTON BENDISH

Also known as Eastmoor landing ground, this site, covering about 340 acres, was established in 1939 as a satellite for Marham, about 4 miles north-east. Several Hawker Hurricanes of 56 Operational Training Unit (OTU) at Sutton Bridge were occasionally dispersed at Barton Bendish in the early war-years. From September 1939 twelve Wellingtons of 38, 115 and later 218 Squadron were dispersed here and were refuelled and rearmed at Marham. Ground crews were transported back and forth by road, although some were carried in the Wellingtons. To conceal them from the air, the tails of the Wellingtons were moved under bordering beech trees. (When the satellite was not required for flying, large pipes were laid across the landing ground and large fields in the area had trenches dug to prevent enemy aircraft from landing.) On 5 November 1939, with overcast at 400 feet and rain showers, the 38 Squadron crews flew their aircraft from Marham to Barton Bendish at low level. A Wellington I flown by veteran pilot Sergeant. E. T. 'Slim' Summers AFM struck a tree and crashed at Boughton killing him and six ground crew who were on board to service the aircraft on arrival at Barton Bendish.

Early in 1940 four Wellingtons of the New Zealand Flight were stored at Barton Bendish. On 20 November 1940 a Wellington Ic of 38 Squadron flown by Sergeant I. N. Robertson, made a belly-landing there, having failed to maintain height on take-off during a non-operational flight. The aircraft was repaired on site and returned to service. During this period the airfield was used as a decoy site with a flarepath in operation at night. From June to September 1941 detachments of 26 and 268 (Army Co-operation) Squadrons were stationed at Barton Bendish with Curtis Tomahawk IIa low-level reconnaissance aircraft and a number of Westland Lysanders. No.218 Conversion Flight followed with Wellingtons, before moving to Oakington on 2 October 1942. In 1942 Downham Market opened as Marham's satellite in place of Barton Bendish, which was unsuitable for 218 CU's Stirlings. (See also, Wellington: *The Geodetic Giant* by Martin Bowman.)

BIRCHAM NEWTON

This was one of the longest-serving RAF aerodromes in East Anglia, with a history stretching back to the First World War. After hosting several bomber squadrons throughout the inter-war years Bircham was transferred to Coastal Command (16 Group). On 22 May 1939 the station held an Empire Day open day and air display. About 5,000 people enjoyed a 4½ hour programme, which included Ansons and Wellingtons bombing a target in the middle of the aerodrome, an aerobatic display by a Miles Magister, an Avro Tutor bursting balloons released from the ground and three Hawker Henleys towing drogue targets. During the summer of 1939 'C' and 'B' Flights of 1 Anti-Aircraft Co-operation Unit arrived with Hawker Henley target tugs to give the gunners at Weybourne more realistic practice.

A dozen Blenheim IFs of 26 and 601 Squadrons were detached to Bircham Newton for a raid on the German submarine base at Borkum on 7 November 1939 and all returned safely to land in Essex. No.220 Squadron left for Thornaby in August and 42 Squadron arrived from Thorney Island with Vildebeest IV biplane torpedo-bombers for convoy escort and fishery protection duties. In early 1940 42 Squadron re-equipped with Beaufort Is at North Coates and were engaged in minelaying in enemy and home waters. During this time, the only aircraft available for fishery patrols at Bircham Newton were an Avro Anson and a Percival Gull.

In January 1940 'D' Flight of 233 Squadron with Blenheim IVs arrived to protect coastal shipping and formed into 'B' Flight of 254 Squadron which had arrived on 28 January. On 4 March 2 General Reconnaissance Unit (GRU) was formed with 5 Wellington DWI (directional wireless installation) aircraft, each with a degaussing hoop fitted for anti-magnetic mine patrols. No.2 GRU soon moved to Manston in Kent. Also in March Hudsons began to replace the Ansons of 206 Squadron which had been stationed at Bircham since August 1936. On 24 April 254 Squadron departed for Scotland, their place being taken by 235 Squadron flying Blenheim Ifs and IVfs for convoy and escort duties. On 7 May 825 Squadron Fleet Air Arm (FAA) arrived from Ford with Fairey Albacore I torpedo bombers. No.815 Squadron FAA also arrived for a short stay, leaving for Ford with their Swordfish I aircraft on 5 June.

From 1940 onwards units stationed at Bircham used the

A number of units were stationed in Norfolk with Hawker Henley TT.III two-seat target tugs, which were fitted with a windmill device on the port side of the rear cockpit that was turned by the slipstream and wound in the drogue target after firing practice. During the summer of 1939 1 AACU arrived at Bircham Newton to give the gunners at Weybourne more realistic practice. 1 AACU had a detachment at Langham from July 1940 to 1 November 1942. From December 1943 to August 1945 695 Squadron was equipped with Henley III and other aircraft at Bircham Newton. (*BAe*)

satellite airfields of Langham and Docking. In June detachments of 229 Squadron were stationed there with Hurricane Is to provide fighter cover until September, when the Battle of Britain was drawing to a close. On 5 September, 'K' Flight of 1 Anti-Aircraft Co-operation Unit arrived with Henley target tugs and later received a few Battle target tugs. In November 1940 403 Meteorological Flight was formed with a few Blenheims and on the 21st 221 Squadron was formed with Wellington Ia and Ic aircraft for anti-submarine patrol, convoy-escort and shipping-reconnaissance sorties. The same day 252 Squadron formed as Coastal Command's first Beaufighter squadron and after working up moved in December to Chivenor.

On 26 January 1941 HM King George VI and HM Queen Elizabeth and the two princesses inspected the station and its aircraft. The King presented decorations and awards to several aircrew stationed at Bircham and other aerodromes, including two of Coltishall's fighter pilots. Squadron Leader Robert Stanford Tuck, 257 'Burma' Squadron Commanding Officer (CO) received the DSO and a bar to his DFC and Flight Lieutenant Brian van Mentz of 222 Squadron received the DFC he was awarded in October, the citation crediting him with 6 victories and 3 probables over France and England. (*See also Coltishall and Horning*)

On 10 February 1941 53 Squadron arrived from Thorney Island for a few days with Blenheim IVs. In early 1941 403 Met Flight received a few Hudsons to supplement the Blenheims, while on 1 March it was renumbered 1403 Met Flight. In May 1941 221 Squadron left for Northern Ireland, while 206 Squadron went to St Eval. No.200 Squadron was re-formed on 25 May 1941, receiving Hudson IVs the following month, before leaving for Bathurst in the Gambia to begin operations. No.500 Squadron arrived on 30 May to replace 235 Squadron, operating their Blenheim IVs on coastal patrols and anti-shipping strikes before conversion to the Hudson. (On 16 January 1942 a Hudson of 500 Squadron crashed near Lowlands Farm, Bacton, during a snowstorm. Local people made a rescue attempt but the crew of four was killed. A cairn marks the site of the crash.)

In June 248 Squadron arrived from Scotland with Blenheim IVs, soon after re-equipping with Beaufighter Ics and using them in the anti-shipping and convoy-escort role. On 30 June 608 Squadron arrived with Blenheims, converting the following month to Hudson III and V aircraft before departing in December 1941. At about the same time 'K' and 'M' Flights of 1 Anti-Aircraft Co-operation Unit moved to Langham. From June to December 1941 detachments of 59 Squadron were at Bircham with Blenheims and Hudsons, while in September, a detachment of 248 Squadron left, followed in early 1942 by the rest of the squadron. On 29 October 1941 1401 Met Flight arrived with a few Blenheims and Gladiators. No.279 Squadron was formed at Bircham Newton as an air-sea rescue (ASR) unit on 15 November flying a few Hudsons and Ansons specially equipped with smoke floats, marine markers, signalling equipment and dinghies.

On 22 January 1942 279 (ASR) Squadron became operational, becoming the first unit to carry airborne lifeboats. From September to November the squadron operated a single Albemarle for evaluation in the ASR role. (No.407 Squadron moved to St Eval on 1 October and early in November 279 left for Thornaby.) On 31 March 407 Squadron Royal Canadian Air Force (RCAF) arrived with Hudsons, followed on 24 April by 320 (Dutch) Squadron, also flying Hudsons. By May aircrew of 407 Squadron had been awarded two DSOs, two DFCs and three DFMs. Between 30 April and 31 May the squadron attacked 83,000 tons of enemy shipping. No.1401 Met Flight received a few Hudsons in May. No.311 (Czech) Squadron of Coastal Command was stationed at Bircham Newton with Wellington Is for the third 1,000-bomber raid on the night of 25/26 June, when the target was Bremen. That same night the Hudsons of 320 and 407 Squadrons made diversionary anti-shipping raids. In July 1401 and 1403 Met Flights were disbanded and re-formed the next day as 521 (Met) Squadron. The Swordfish of 819 Squadron FAA left for Thorney Island on 8 September after a short stay. On 9 October Swordfish of 812 Squadron FAA arrived from Docking, staying until 3 November when the squadron moved to Hatston.

Between February 1943 and May 1944 a detachment of 409 Squadron RCAF was stationed at Bircham with Beaufighter II and VI nightfighters and Mosquito XIII aircraft later. These were sometimes flown on Rangers, attacking enemy night fighters over Europe. On 31 March 1943 521 Squadron disbanded and split into 1401 and 1409 (Met) Flights. The latter left for Oakington on 1 April. Between 17 March and 28 April 53 Squadron was stationed at Bircham Newton with Whitley aircraft, flying only nine patrols before moving to Thorney Island to re-equip with Liberators. The Warwick Training Unit was formed at Bircham Newton and Docking on 28 June to train Coastal Command crews for this new type of air-sea rescue aircraft. The unit left for Thornaby in late November. By mid-1943 more than 100 enemy vessels had been sunk or badly damaged by Bircham-stationed aircraft.

In March 320 (Dutch) Squadron transferred to 2 Group Bomber Command and moved to Methwold to convert to the Mitchell. 415 'Swordfish' Squadron RCAF arrived on 15 November with Wellington GRXIII and Albacore I aircraft, using these on night anti-shipping sorties off the Dutch coast and anti-E and R-boat patrols. (The Canadians also laid smoke screens on D-Day and in July 1944 they transferred to Bomber Command.) On 1 December 1943 695 Squadron re-formed from 1611 and 1612 (Target Tug) Flights and flew various types on anti-aircraft co-operation duties over East Anglia moving in August 1945 to Horsham St Faith.

In the spring of 1944 2 Armament Practice Camp arrived with Martinets, moving to Docking on 29 August. During that summer the Coastal Command Preparation Pool (CCPP) was formed to evaluate various aircraft and their armament. In July 524 Squadron arrived with Wellington GRXIII aircraft for anti-E-boat and shipping patrols. This unit moved to the satellite airfield at Langham the following October. The Avengers of 855 Squadron FAA arrived on 6 September, operating mainly at night from Docking on anti-shipping patrols until 17 October, when the squadron moved to Lee-on-Solent. In late September 119 and 819 Squadrons FAA arrived with Albacores and Swordfish respectively to begin training for night anti-submarine patrols. Swordfish aircraft began to replace the Albacores of 119 Squadron in January 1945. The same month 119 and 819 Squadrons FAA left for Belgium, where they flew patrols at night searching for midget submarines and E- and R-boats. For night operations the aircraft were painted black overall. On 27 February 1945 819 Squadron returned to Bircham to disband, as did 119 Squadron in May 1945.

On 11 August 1945 Bircham was transferred to Fighter Command, in 1946 it changed to Transport Command, and a year later it transferred to RAF Technical Training Command. On 18 December 1962 about 300 people attended the closing ceremony of RAF Bircham Newton. The Central Band of the RAF and the Queen's Colour Squadron beat retreat with a lone bugler sounding the 'Last Post'. The reviewing officer was Air Marshal Sir Alfred Earle, AOC-in-Chief, Technical Training Command, and other VIPs present included Air Marshals Lord Portal (ex-CO of 7 Squadron in 1927) and Lord Tedder (ex-CO of 207 Squadron 1920–22.) Since 1966 Bircham has become the location for the Industry Training Board, now National Construction College (East).

BODNEY

Fear of a concentrated attack by the enemy on any of the permanent RAF airfields in East Anglia led in 1939–40 to several remote locations being considered as possible satellite airfields so that aircraft and facilities could be more widespread and less liable to attack. RAF Watton, like many others in the region, was one of the stations built during the pre-war expansion period, and its hangars and airfield were an open invitation to *Luftwaffe* raiders, so a large square grass field at Bodney in Breckland 7 miles to the south-west was selected as a landing ground for its Blenheims of 21 and 82 Squadrons. A number of huts were erected on the northern side of the landing ground for administration and technical services and some local housing was requisitioned for barrack use while tented accommodation was used until more permanent buildings could be built to house up to 1,709 men. Some woodland was removed and a perimeter track was laid with short spurs leading to large circular dispersal pads beneath fir trees in the surrounding woods. The grass-surface runways were north-east–south-west 1,000 yards long; and north-west–south-east and east–west, both 900 yards long. The landing ground was declared operational in March 1940 when some Blenheim IVs of 82 Squadron, and later 21 Squadron began using Bodney. During the fighting in France in May 1940 Blenheims using the landing ground flew on operations with crews from its parent station at Watton as the RAF and BEF fought alongside their French and Belgian allies in a vain attempt to stem the German *Blitzkrieg*. Losses were high and the worst disaster to befall 82 Squadron occurred on 13 August 1940 when six Blenheim crews of 'B' Flight at Bodney joined six crews of 'A' Flight from Watton in a suicidal attack on Aalborg airfield in

Blenheim IV R3800 UX-Z of 82 Squadron hidden beneath the trees at Great Wood, Bodney during the summer of 1940. Flown by Flight Lieutenant T. E. Syms, R3800 failed to return on 13 August 1940 when it was hit by flak and fell blazing into Limfjord, 50 yards offshore by Aalborg See, the *Luftwaffe* seaplane base at Aalborg. Sergeant Wright survived. Sergeant F. V. Turner was killed. (*Wartime Watton Museum*)

Denmark, occupied by Ju 88s of I/JG30, which were making sporadic raids on Scotland and northern England. One Blenheim returned early low on fuel and the remaining eleven aircraft were all shot down by flak and Bf 109Es of V/JG77 from Stavanger-Sola.

Bodney continued to be used by squadrons from Watton throughout 1941. On occasion German night intruders were attracted by the gooseneck flare path, which was lit to guide returning Blenheims. On 11/12 February 1941 when the Blenheims were returning from a raid on Hanover, *Oberleutnant* Paul Semrau of I/NJG2 flying a Ju 88C followed Squadron Leader J. S. Sabine's Blenheim back. Unable to land and short of fuel the Blenheim was attacked and it crashed. Semrau then shot down Blenheim Z5877 flown by Sergeant A. Chatterway, who was circling the airfield, awaiting his turn to land. Chatterway was killed, his observer, Pilot Officer Cherval was seriously wounded and the wireless operator/air gunner (WOp/AG), Sergeant Burch was wounded in the leg. (Major Semrau scored forty-six night victories and was awarded the *Ritterkreuz* with *Eichenlab.*

Landing at Twente airfield on 8 February 1945 he was shot down and killed by a 402 Squadron Spitfire.)

On 13 April eleven of 61 Squadron's Hampdens were repositioned to Watton for cloud-cover daylight raids over the Continent under 2 Group control. The first sorties were flown from Bodney on 18 April by six Hampdens against the docks at Cherbourg. One was hit by anti-aircraft fire and the wounded pilot and his crew baled out near Swindon. This aircraft (AD825) was the only Hampden lost in action from a sortie from East Anglia. On 30 April 61 Squadron returned to 5 Group.

Because of high losses it was decided in August 1940 to withdraw most of the Blenheims from daylight operations and to employ them in night attacks, initially on the Channel ports in support of the heavies of Bomber Command. During the bitterly cold winter of 1941 Blenheim squadrons such as 82 at Bodney continued flying night operations and equally suicidal daylight attacks on German shipping off the enemy coasts and other targets further inland. One of the biggest 2 Group operations occurred on 12 August when fifty-six Blenheim crews flew to Cologne and made spirited attacks on two power stations there. Twenty-year-old Pilot Officer Walter Robinson, whose crew joined 82 Squadron at Bodney on 5 August 1941, recalls:

My navigator/bomb aimer was Pilot Officer Kenneth Pike and the wireless operator/air gunner Sergeant Douglas Attenborough. On the afternoon of 11 August the nine aircraft of our squadron flew to Watton for briefing and to take off together with 21 Squadron the next day. We did not as yet know the target but had an inkling that a big operation was planned. The starboard engine of my Blenheim (T2122) lost power during the short flight to Watton and I made a single-engine landing. As a newcomer to the squadron I was assigned the oldest and most worn out aircraft, as was the custom. This particular plane had already been giving trouble. The engineering flight sergeant at Watton guaranteed, however, to have it back on top form for the next day. After spending the night at our officers' quarters near Bodney we returned to Watton early the next morning for briefing. We were to fly in loose vics of three aircraft, at a maximum height of 50 feet. Our route would take us across Holland and into Germany. Upon approaching Cologne we would split into two sections, one

Ground crews at Bodney stop for tea break at the Church Army tea wagon provided by the 'people of Uganda to the people of Britain'. (*Watton Wartime Museum*)

> *to bomb the Knapsack power station and the other that at Quadrath. Other squadrons were, of course involved but we knew nothing of their routes.*

Attenborough adds, 'The CO seeing us off on the Cologne "do" said: "For those of you that get back, I'll have a good lunch waiting for you". Being my first op I thought, "What the hell am I doing here!'

Robinson's crew made it back to Bodney in their battered Blenheim by the skin of their teeth and arrived at 1.30 p.m. 'just the right time for the CO's sumptuous lunch!' In all, twelve Blenheims were lost on 12 August and many more returned home badly damaged (see *Blenheim Strike* by Theo Boiten). Unescorted operations cost many Blenheim crews their lives for little benefit to the war effort. When on 26 August 2 Group dispatched thirty-nine Blenheims on coastal sweeps and a Circus raid, seven Blenheims were lost. Four of the losses were from 82 Squadron during an unescorted sweep in the Heligoland Bight and they included the new CO, Wing Commander Lascelles DFC, a cousin of the Royal Family.

In November 1941 the daylight anti-shipping campaign ceased and the Blenheims were switched to equally unsuitable night-intruding operations against German airfields on the Continent.

(If a pilot got into difficulty at 1,000 or 1,500 feet – the height they were expected to fly for intruding – the low speed (180 mph) and the rate of climb (400 feet per minute) made it difficult to change altitude and direction quickly enough to throw off searchlights and flak.) No.82 Squadron was the first unit to finish night-intruder training late in December and six crews flew the first operation on the 27th to Soesterberg airfield, where sixty Do 217 bombers were based. Wing Commander D. J. A. Roe DFC successfully led the crews to Soesterberg in the early evening and in the circuit two Blenheims engaged Dorniers with machine-guns and then all the crews dropped their bombs on the airfield. All six returned safely. The Blenheims from Watton and Bodney flew only a few more night sorties to the Netherlands during the last days of 1941 before winter set in. During operations between May 1940 and March 1942, thirty-four Blenheims were missing in action, twenty-seven of which were from 82 Squadron. Ten more were lost in operational crashes.

Early in 1942 it was planned to re-equip 21 Squadron with Boeing Flying Fortress I aircraft, which had begun arriving in Britain from the USA in April. This would have involved taking a first-line squadron off operations so on 7 May 90 Squadron was officially re-formed at Watton under the command of 2 Group and four days later the squadron took delivery of two B-17Cs. On 12 May flying training began at Bodney but it proved only a short sojourn, lasting only two days, for the undulating grass landing ground proved most unsuitable for a heavy aircraft such as the Fortress. However, the first Fortress flight on conversion to type was made from the remote Norfolk airfield on the 13th. Two days later training flights were resumed at Great Massingham, while the Fortresses went for overhaul at West Raynham. No.21 Squadron, meanwhile, had sent a detachment to Malta and disbanded at Luqa on 14 March. It was re-formed at Bodney that same day and for a short time flew Blenheims prior to receiving Lockheed Vega Ventura aircraft. (Two other Ventura squadrons, 487 RNZAF and 464 RAAF were formed at Feltwell in August and September respectively.) No.21 Squadron remained at Bodney until October, finally moving to Methwold, where Ventura operations began on 3 November.

During 1942, while still in use as a relief landing ground for training aircraft from Watton, Bodney's facilities were gradually improved to enable the airfield to be allocated to the USAAF for development into a Class A standard bomber base. Five blister hangars and two T2 hangars, one on the technical site in a wood on the west side and the other on a dispersal spur on the southern side, were erected. Aircraft could now be dispersed to eight small asphalt pans and four blind strips and fifteen large asphalt pans grouped in threes around the landing ground. Bomb stores were located ¾ mile south of the airfield by the River Wissey. To the south-east one communal and four domestic sites were dispersed and to the north along the road to Little Cressingham there were three domestic sites, a communal site and sick quarters. Accommodation was provided for 190 officers and 1,519 enlisted men. However Bodney was not further developed as a bomber station and in June it became instead a USAAF fighter base and was now known as Station 141. (The runways remained grass but PSP matting was laid in late 1943 at some of the hardstandings.)

In July 1942 the 352nd Fighter Group, whose three squadrons were equipped with P-47D Thunderbolts, arrived. In August room had to be found for no less than seventy-five Thunderbolts on the compact airfield. The group flew its first mission on 9 September when it provided withdrawal cover for the heavies, before taking part in numerous escorts and patrols in support of 8th Air Force Bomber formations. In October 1943 the 352nd became a part of the 67th Fighter Wing. On 25 November they provided cover for the first P-47 fighter-bomber raid when Thunderbolts attacked St Omer/Fort Rouge airfield in northern France. In April 1944 the 352nd Fighter Group converted to P-51D and K Mustangs (with blue noses for identification). For the remainder of the war the 'Blue-nosed Bastards of Bodney' flew escorts for the bombers, being awarded a Distinguished Unit Citation for the raid on Brunswick on 8 May 1944. On D-Day they supported the cross-Channel operation and then carried out ground-strafing and dive-bombing operations during the breakout at St-Lô. In September they supported the Market-Garden operation at Arnhem.

In December 1944 with the German breakthrough in the Ardennes most of the group's P-51s moved to Asch, Belgium, to provide cover for 9th Air Force fighter-bomber operations. During one of these missions it lost Captain George Preddy, the leading P-51 ace, who was killed after being brought down near Liège by American light AA fire. On 28 January 1945 the 352nd moved to Chièvres, Belgium before returning to Bodney in early

Shirt-sleeved fitters carry out a double engine change to a Blenheim IV at Bodney on a warm summer's day in 1940. (*Wartime Watton Museum*)

April. (Earlier, on the night of 4 March a Ju 88 had dropped two 250kg bombs on the airfield.) The 352nd flew its final mission on 3 May 1945.

On 3 November 1945 the 352nd Fighter Group officially vacated Bodney and left for America and on the 8th the airfield passed to 12 Group, RAF Fighter Command and became, briefly, Hethel's satellite. Closure came on 26 November 1945 when it was taken over by the War Office. The airfield was closed to flying and following some government use of the domestic sites these were gradually demolished. In later years the site was absorbed into the nearby Stanford Training Area (STANTA) for use by the British Army.

COLTISHALL

This famous airfield was constructed as a bomber station in February 1939 to standardized 'Expansion Period' designs, said to have been the brainchild of Sir Edward Lutyens, with five C-Type hangars and a grass airfield. However, the disastrous air campaign in France in 1940 resulted in Coltishall becoming a fighter airfield as bomber stations in the region were now a prime target for *Luftwaffe* bombers and Duxford was the only fighter station available to protect the eastern region. Coltishall opened in May 1940 as a part of 12 Group Fighter Command. The first fighters arrived on 29 May – a detachment of Spitfire Is of 66 Squadron from Watton, which was being used as an advanced landing ground for Duxford. Coltishall's station commander found in early June, 'No squadrons, few officers and very few airmen'. Later that month the battered remnants of 242 Squadron flying Hurricane Is arrived. It was comprised mainly of Canadian pilots who, after their mauling in the Battle of France, were feeling very sorry for themselves and it was felt that they needed a gutsy leader to raise morale and rebuild the squadron. No less a man than thirty-year-old Squadron Leader Douglas Bader, who

Squadron Leader Bader (centre) in September 1940 with Pilot Officer William Lidstone McKnight DFC (killed in action 12 January 1941, seventeen victories) to his right and Flight Lieutenant George Eric Ball DFC (killed in a flying accident 1 February 1946, to his left. (*IWM*)

had artificial legs following a tragic crash while stunting in a Bulldog on 14 December 1931, arrived to take command. (In June 1943 Flying Officer John 'Hoppy' Hodgkinson of 611 Squadron FAA was at Coltishall. Like Bader he had lost both his legs as the result of a flying accident.) Bader had been invalided out of the RAF in May 1933 but by sheer persistence he fought his way back to flying and he scored the first of twenty wartime victories on 1 June 1940 over Dunkirk. Bader's strong leadership won over his new pilots and he made sure 242 was re-equipped by cutting through the red tape so that the squadron was soon operational again.

No.66 Squadron, commanded by Rupert Leigh, a close friend and old Cranwell chum of Bader's, and 242 Squadron's Hurricanes were called into action on 10 July. Off Winterton 66 Squadron claimed one of the first official victories of the Battle of Britain when Sergeant Fred N. Robertson, flying a Spitfire I, claimed a Do 17Z of II/KG3. (Robertson, whose claim was reduced to a ⅓ kill with two others, was killed on the night of 31 August 1943 when he collided with a B-17 near Norwich.) No.242 Squadron's Hurricanes tussled with He 111H-2s of III/KG53 and Sub Lieutenant Richard E. Gardner destroyed one of the bombers, which pancaked into the sea off Lowestoft. Next day Squadron Leader Bader claimed his second victory, a Dornier Do 17Z off Cromer. It was the first of eleven victories Bader scored while leading 242 before he was promoted to Wing Commander Flying of the Tangmere Wing in March 1941. Bader was awarded a DFC in January 1941 on reaching ten victories.

By August 1940 the Battle of Britain was passing Coltishall by but 12 Group's 'Big Wing' formation was born and the Coltishall squadrons became fully involved. Bader was convinced that the 'Big Wing' was the most effective method of attack, involving as it did a minimum of three fighter squadrons operating from stations in the region and to the north of London from Duxford. On 30 August the 'Big Wing' claimed 7 Bf 110s (two falling to Bader) and three Heinkel He 111s without loss. On 7 September 1940 Pilot Officer Denis Crowley-Milling of 242 Squadron was shot down near Chelmsford after claiming a Bf 110 over London. He went on to serve with distinction and retired with the rank of Air Marshal.

In September Pilot Officer James E. 'Johnnie' Johnson arrived at Coltishall with fellow pilots from 19 Squadron at Duxford to report to 616 (South Yorkshire) Squadron Auxiliary Air Force (AAF), which had been pulled out of the front line to re-form. Johnson, who by the end of the war was the highest-scoring Allied fighter pilot of the European conflict with thirty-four victories and seven shared, reported to the squadron commander, Squadron Leader H. F. 'Billy' Burton, who explained that whilst at RAF Kenley 616 Squadron's causalities had been high. No.66 Squadron continued with shipping patrols off the east coast. One Saturday in September Johnson and his fellow pilots drove into Norwich and were wedged into the stuffy bar of the Bell when the RAF police arrived and announced that all RAF personnel were to report to their units immediately. At Coltishall they discovered that Alert No.1, 'invasion imminent and probable invasion within 12 hours', had been declared. Any apprehension that Johnson and his fellow pilots may have felt was quickly dispelled when Johnson almost collided with Douglas Bader in the mess, which was in an otherwise confused state. Bader said, 'I say, old boy, what's all the flap about?' 'I don't really know, sir,' replied Johnson, 'But there are reports of enemy landings.' Bader pushed open the swing doors and stalked into the noisy, confused atmosphere of the anteroom. He took in the scene and then demanded in a loud voice and in choice, fruity language, what all the panic was about. Half a dozen voices started to explain and as he listened, his eyes swept round the room, lingered for a moment and after a moment's silence whilst he digested the news, bellowed, 'So the bastards are coming. Bloody good show! Think of all those juicy targets on those nice flat beaches. What shooting!' and he made a rude sound with his lips which was meant to be a ripple of machine gun fire. The effect was immediate and extraordinary. Morale soared. On 13 September Douglas Bader was having dinner with his wife Thelma in Coltishall when he received a telephone call informing him of the award of the DSO. On 15 September a much larger 'wing' comprising five squadrons patrolled over London and claimed thirty-two enemy aircraft destroyed and eight damaged, with 242 Squadron claiming twelve of them.

During September the first of several transient squadrons flew into Coltishall when 616 (South Yorkshire) Squadron arrived. The South African fighter ace, Squadron Leader Adolph 'Sailor' Malan, commanded 74 Squadron, which arrived with sixteen Spitfire IIAs on 9 September. On 14 September 74 Squadron claimed a Bf 110 and a Ju 88 off Happisburgh on the Norfolk coast.

The climax of the Battle of Britain was reached on 15 September when 242 Squadron was despatched to Duxford and Bader's pilots destroyed seven enemy bombers and three Bf 109s. During October 64 and 72 Squadrons arrived at Coltishall and on the 20th 242 Squadron left for Duxford. No.72 Squadron damaged a Dornier Do 17 on 27 October when at dusk an He 111H-2 of I/KG1 attacked Coltishall and machine-gunned one of the many defence posts. The raider escaped but coastal defences hit the aircraft and it ditched off Clacton. On

Wing Commander Howard Peter 'Cowboy' Blatchford DFC RCAF, a popular Canadian from Alberta and OC Coltishall Wing. (*Mick Jennings Collection*)

8 November eleven bombs fell on Coltishall, causing considerable damage to the watch office. Nuisance raids like this highlighted the vulnerability of placing fighters in a single area and the satellite airfield at Matlaske came into its own.

No.222 Squadron arrived at Coltishall on 11 November to replace 64 Squadron and on 29 November 72 Squadron departed to Leuchars. Since the departure of 242 Squadron, Hurricanes were few and far between but on 17 December this changed with the arrival of 257 'Burma' Squadron, which was commanded by Squadron Leader Robert 'Bob' Stanford-Tuck DFC. It was stationed at Coltishall for almost twelve months. (On 28 January 1942 Tuck, whose score had risen to twenty-seven victories, was shot down flying a Spitfire over France, and survived to be taken PoW.) By the end of 1940 Coltishall squadrons had claimed eighty-three enemy aircraft destroyed.

During 1941 there was action against enemy aircraft operating off the east coast on 'Kipper' patrols which were mounted to protect the North Sea fishing fleets from *Luftwaffe* attention. When weather and cloud conditions were favourable Coltishall's Hurricanes went on low-level fighter sweeps over the Dutch coast attacking targets of opportunity in what became known as Rhubarbs.

On 8 March 1941 222 Squadron patrolled over Yarmouth, and a Ju 88 which dived through the clouds and dropped four bombs in the sea off Britannia Pier was shot down by three of the Spitfire pilots and it crashed into the sea off Gorleston. Also during March detachments from 151 Squadron, flying Boulton Paul Defiants, made regular visits to Coltishall on night standbys for patrols over the North Sea. Enemy raids continued in and around Coltishall that month.

On 29 July 1941 another Hurricane unit, 133 Squadron, was formed at Coltishall as the third 'Eagle Squadron' with volunteer American pilots. It did not fly any operational sorties as it was working up to operational readiness prior to a move to Duxford in mid-August. That same month 255 Squadron, which had operated Defiants and Hurricanes at Hibaldstow, Lincolnshire, and was now equipped with the Beaufighter, arrived to provide night-fighter cover to Norwich and the east coast ports while also trialling the new and secret ground controlled interception radar at Neatishead. No.255 Squadron suffered numerous problems with the Beaufighter, which led to many accidents, one of which claimed the CO, Wing Commander S. Bartlett DFC, and his observer. Another Beaufighter squadron, 604 (County of Middlesex) Squadron at Middle Wallop, Hampshire, had a permanent detachment at Coltishall to cover the eastern sector

RAF Coltishall in 1946.
(*RAF Coltishall*)

whilst 255 Squadron worked up to operational readiness. No.604 Squadron was the top-scoring night fighter squadron in the RAF and was commanded by Wing Commander John 'Cats Eyes' Cunningham DSO DFC. On 22 August Cunningham and his navigator, Pilot Officer C. P. Rawnsley, destroyed a Heinkel He 111 of VIII/KG40 35 miles north-west of Coltishall. On 1 September they destroyed a Junkers Ju 88, which fell into the sea and exploded 25 miles east of Winterton. No.604 Squadron returned to Middle Wallop in September and the now fully operational 255 Squadron succeeded them. No.257 Squadron moved to Honiley in Warwickshire on 1 November. (That same month a second satellite airfield was opened at Ludham to relieve the pressure on Coltishall and Matlaske.) On 8 November 137 Squadron arrived from Charmy Down, Somerset, with twin-engined Westland Whirlwind I fighters. Squadron Leader H. St John Coghlan DFC's squadron began operations with coastal patrols and convoy escorts almost immediately off Yarmouth and the east coast. On 1 December the Whirlwinds moved to Matlaske to continue operations.

In February 1942 when the 'Channel Dash' of the German battleships *Scharnhorst* and *Gneisenau* occurred, fourteen Beauforts of 42 Squadron were rushed south from Leuchars to intercept them, but having been turned away from Bircham Newton because of snow, the aircraft diverted to Coltishall. Three of the aircraft, supposedly loaded with torpedoes, were found on arrival to be unarmed and two others developed technical faults. When eventually the enemy vessels were found off the Hook of Holland six of the Beauforts attacked with torpedoes without success. No.86 Squadron arrived at Coltishall with Beauforts to try again but the battleships had by now sailed to the north-east, well out of range.

In March 1942 when 2 Group resumed its daylight offensive with Bostons from Swanton Morley, Oulton and Great Massingham, Coltishall's Spitfires escorted all the operations from advanced airfields. March also saw the departure of 255 Squadron to High Ercall, and 68 Squadron, which was also equipped with Beaufighters, replaced them. The squadron was largely made up of Czech personnel, who were commanded by Wing Commander Max Aitken DFC, the son of Lord Beaverbrook. The squadron became actively involved in the development and trials of radar and greatly assisted Wing

Commander D. A. Jackson of the Telecommunications Research Establishment, which was at an advanced stage in the testing of AI Mk IX airborne intercept radar. On 23 December 1942 Wing Commander Jackson and Dr Downing, a physicist responsible for much of the radar design and construction, acted as radar operators aboard two Beaufighters from Coltishall to monitor the performance of the AI Mk IX. As they approached the target area a Spitfire piloted by a Canadian on his first operational sortie attacked and shot the Beaufighter down over the sea, killing Downing and his pilot. The other Beaufighter was badly damaged but made it back to Coltishall.

On 23 July 68 Squadron claimed five of the seven victories over East Anglia and resulted in the award of the DSO to Wing Commander Aitken, who now had fourteen enemy aircraft destroyed. The Free Czech Government presented him with the War Cross. Also during July Mustangs of 268 Squadron at Snailwell often used Coltishall for refuelling and rearming prior to and after shipping-reconnaissance sorties, or Lagoons, as they were more commonly known. Squadrons in 12 Group were involved in the raid on Dieppe and at Coltishall Wing Commander Jameson led aircraft from 411, 483 and 610 Squadrons in support of the operation on 19 August. Three Fw 190s and two Bf 109s were claimed destroyed for the loss of three Spitfires. On 24 August a Havoc of 1433 Flight at Wittering arrived at Coltishall for three days to carry out ground-control sorties. The aircraft was fitted with AI Mk IV radar and in the nose was a 2,700 million-candlepower Helmore-Turbinlite, the batteries of which were housed in the bomb bay. In theory the Turbinlite Havoc would illuminate a target and an accompanying fighter would attack and shoot it down. The Havoc could easily have used the AI to close in and shoot down its target and eventually the Tubinlite Havoc Flights were disbanded.

During the first week of October 1942 American airmen gathered at Coltishall to form the 346th Fighter Squadron (FS) of the 350th Fighter Group, 8th Fighter Command. Some of the pilots came from the 31st and 52nd Fighter Groups equipped with Spitfire Vs and the others were former Eagle Squadron pilots. Like those of the 345th FS at Duxford and the 347th FS at Snailwell, they were to train in the ground attack role on the P-400 Airacobra before moving to North Africa as part of the *Torch* invasion in November. Most of the P-400s were still in their crates at various depots throughout England and the air depot failed to meet the planned assembly deadline and delivery of additional aircraft. On 6 November Second Lieutenant Harley J. Greenway was killed when his aircraft crashed on take-off from Coltishall. Two days later the invasion of North Africa took place without the 52nd Fighter Group. In mid-December twenty-five new Airacobras were acquired and on 2 January 1943 the Americans moved to Portreath in Cornwall before flying to North Africa.

In the meanwhile, Swordfish and Albacore biplanes of 841 Squadron Fleet Air Arm had arrived at Coltishall in the later part of December 1942 and up until July 1943 these aircraft were used by Detachment 3 of the squadron on night searches and attacks against enemy submarines and E-Boats operating off the east coast. Another detachment at Coltishall during the same period was the Mandrel Screen Unit, part of 515 Squadron at Hunsdon, with Boulton Paul Defiant IIs. Mandrel was an airborne device

No.602 Squadron operated from Coltishall from 30 September to 18 October 1944 flying escort and strike sorties over the Continent. This Spitfire IX with Johnnie McMahon in the cockpit is fitted with a 90-gallon slipper tank under the fuselage. No.602 Squadron also operated from Matlaske from 18 October to 20 November 1944 and from Ludham from 23 February to 5 April 1945 before returning to Coltishall 9 April to 15 May 1945. (*Mick Jennings Collection*)

used to jam enemy early-warning radar. At first bad weather hampered operations but by March fifty-eight Mandrel sorties had been flown. Night Ranger sorties were also continually being flown by Mosquitoes of 25 Squadron, who used Coltishall as a forward-operating location from their home station at Church Fenton.

On 2 May 1943 118 Squadron's Spitfires escorted Venturas of 464 Squadron Royal Australian Air Force (RAAF) in an attack on the Royal Dutch Steel works at Ijmuiden, but the target escaped damage and a further raid was scheduled for the next day by Boston IIIAs. As a diversion, twelve Venturas of 487 Squadron Royal New Zealand Air Force (RNZAF) at Methwold, led by Squadron Leader Leonard Trent DFC, were to bomb the Amsterdam power station. The Venturas flew to Coltishall and rendezvoused with their Spitfire Vb escorts of 118, 167 and 504 Squadrons led by Wing Commander Howard Peter 'Cowboy' Blatchford DFC, a popular Canadian from Alberta and officer commanding (OC) Coltishall Wing. One Ventura aborted *en route* and was the only aircraft to return to Methwold. The Spitfires had their hands full and an Fw 190A hit 'Cowboy' Blatchford. He ditched 40 miles off Mundesley on the Norfolk coast at about 1815 hours. His body was never found. Spitfires of 118 and 167 Squadrons claimed three enemy fighters but the Fw 190s and Bf 109s picked off all the eleven Venturas in just a matter of minutes. Last to fall was Trent's aircraft, which went into a spin and broke up. Two crew died trapped inside but Trent and another crew member were hurled out to survive and become PoWs. It was only after he was repatriated that the full story became known and on 1 March 1946 Trent was awarded the VC for his leadership and gallantry (See *The Reich Intruders* by Martin W. Bowman).

A Handley Page Halifax and an Avro Lancaster at Coltishall after diverting there following a raid on the Reich. Coltishall's nearness to the Norfolk coast made it a welcome and safe haven for aircraft in an emergency. (*Mick Jennings Collection*)

During 1943 Beaufighter IF detachments from 409 Squadron were sent to Coltishall for Ranger sorties over the Continent, as were Beaufighter FVIs from Wittering equipped with Serrate homer and AI Mk IV radar for bomber support operations. No.891 Squadron FAA made nightly anti-E-Boat sorties and Spitfires, Typhoons and Mosquitoes continued flying strikes against enemy targets. In 1944 squadrons came and went. On 5 February, 68 Squadron, with a score of seventy enemy aircraft, moved out, having been at Coltishall since March 1942, their place being taken by 25 Squadron commanded by Wing Commander Wight-Boycott, DSO. From April to the end of 1944 Spitfire PRIIs and PRXIXs of 541 Squadron from RAF Benson used Coltishall as a stepping stone for sorties over Europe. Also in April 611 Squadron, which had been at Coltishall since 25 September 1943 and 64 Squadron, which arrived on 1 July 1943 left and 316 Squadron with Mustang IIIs, the first of the Polish Squadrons at Coltishall arrived. They moved to West Malling, Kent to attack V-1s over the Channel.

On 14 August 1944 the first operation by Czech fighter pilots flying from Britain over German territory took place when 312 Squadron took off from Coltishall to carry out a fighter sweep over the Ruhr in conjunction with the Spitfires of 229 Squadron. In September 25 and 409 Squadron's Mosquitoes claimed their first Heinkel He 111H-22 V-1-carrying aircraft in the North Sea. In November Mosquito NFXXIXs and NFXVIIs of 68 and 125 Squadrons scored further victories against the V-1 carriers. Between September 1944 and January 1945 881 V-1s were plotted, of which, 387 were destroyed, seventy by fighters. Twenty-six V-1 carriers were also destroyed. The last enemy aircraft to be destroyed near Britain in the Second World War is believed to be a Ju 188 10 miles north-east of Cromer by a 125 Squadron Mosquito from Coltishall on 20 March 1945. In all, Coltishall squadrons claimed no less than 207 enemy aircraft destroyed, forty-eight probably destroyed and more than 100 damaged. Fittingly, on 27 July a flying display at the station saw Group Captain Douglas Bader light up the sky in a Spitfire; the first time he had flown since his capture.

After the war the station's front-line status continued unabated with a succession of fighter aircraft. As befits a famous Battle of Britain fighter station, in April 1963 the RAF's Historic Aircraft Flight (HAF) arrived from Horsham St Faith with Hurricane IIC

LF363 and Mk XIX Spitfire PM631. Other Spitfires came and went and a second Hurricane IIc was added. In 1973 Lancaster BI PA474 arrived and the HAF became the Battle of Britain Memorial Flight (BBMF). In March 1976 much to the regret of Norfolk citizens, many thousands of whom attended some truly memorable air shows at 'Colt' during the 1960s the BBMF moved to Coningsby. On 1 April 2006 the last Jaguars joined them at the Lincolnshire. RAF Coltishall closed its gates for the last time on 30 November 2006. It was the last station to have been in continuous use by fighter aircraft since the Battle of Britain.

DOCKING

At the beginning of the Second World War this airfield, which was known locally as Sunderland after a farm on the west side, was the decoy airfield for Bircham Newton, a Coastal Command station 3 miles to the south. A dummy flarepath ('Q' site) ran

From 10 October to 7 November 1942 254 Squadron was at Docking while working up on Torbeaus (Torpedo carrying Beaufighters) prior to joining the North Coates Strike Wing. In April 1944 Langham reopened when a Beaufighter Wing was formed with 455 RAAF and 489 RNZAF Squadrons flying Flakbeau and Torbeau variants. Their main targets were E- and R-boats; flak ships and supply ships off the Dutch and Belgian coasts. (*IWM*)

across the site for night-time use and for daylight use ('K' site) about a dozen dummy Hudsons were deployed. By all accounts it was successful, as the site was bombed several times. From July 1940 Docking became the satellite of Bircham Newton and it was also used as an emergency landing ground. The airfield was grass covered with a concrete peri-track, which can still be used. During 1941 dummy Hurricanes were parked around it to build up the pretence that there was a fighter force in the area.

Between 12 January and 22 February 1942 502 Squadron was stationed at Docking with Whitley GRV aircraft for coastal patrols. No.1401 (Met) Flight was detached from January 1942, using Gladiators and Blenheims for meteorological flights. No.255 Squadron was there from 31 May until 16 July 1942, flying Blenheim IVs in attacks off the Dutch coast. On 27 July 143 Squadron arrived for a one-month stay, flying Blenheims on convoy patrols. That same month 1525 Beam Approach Training Flight moved to Docking with Oxford trainers and remained until May 1945. On 1 August 1942 the 1401 (Met) Flight detachment re-formed as 521 Squadron detachment, adding Mosquito, Hudson and Spitfire aircraft to its strength. From 10 October to 7 November 254 Squadron was at Docking while working up on Torbeaus prior to joining the North Coates Strike Wing. On 10 November 407 Squadron RCAF arrived from St Eval leaving their Hudsons, which had been found to be under-armed when flown against heavily armed convoys. On 6 February 1943 the Canadians moved to Skitton to continue conversion training on Wellingtons.

No.53 Squadron arrived on 17 February 1943 for a one-month stay, converting from the Hudson to the Whitley GRVIII. After working up the squadron moved to Bircham Newton to begin coastal patrols. On 31 March 521 (Met) Squadron disbanded and the detachment at Docking became 1401 (Met) Flight detachment with Gladiators and Hudsons. On 2 April 304 (Polish) Squadron arrived with Wellington Ia and Ic aircraft, using them for anti-E-boat and shipping patrols over the North Sea. It left on 7 June. On 15 April 415 Squadron RCAF arrived with Wellington GRXIII patrol aircraft, flying anti-E-boat and shipping patrols mainly at night off the Dutch coast. The Warwick Training Unit was formed at Docking and Bircham Newton on 28 June, training Coastal Command crews on this new aircraft. The unit moved to Thornaby on 21 November. No.521 Squadron was re-

A Warwick V in flight. The Warwick Training Unit was formed at Bircham Newton and Docking on 28 June 1943 to train Coastal Command crews for this new type of ASR aircraft. The unit left for Thornaby in late November 1943. At Langham 280 Squadron also operated Warwick ASR.Is during September and October 1944, and 1693 Flight operated Warwick ASR.Is from Docking from 31 May to 11 August 1945. (*Charles E. Brown*)

formed at Docking on 1 September from the aircraft of 1401 (Met) Flight, by now flying Hampdens as well as Gladiators and Hudsons. The Hampdens and Hudsons carried out met flights mainly over the North Sea, while the Gladiators were used for local weather flights, often in thick fog. During December Venturas replaced the Hampdens and Hudsons.

In July 1944 415 Squadron was replaced by 524 Squadron, also flying Wellington GRXIII aircraft in the same role; from August the Wellingtons flew mainly from Bircham Newton. Hurricanes supplemented the Gladiators of 521 Squadron from August; the same month No.2 Armament Practice Camp was at Docking for a short period flying Miles Martinet target tugs. In September the Hudsons returned to replace the Venturas and in December some Fortress II and III aircraft arrived for 521 Squadron. By this time some of the aircraft operated from Langham. By the end of the war the squadron was flying only Fortress and Hurricane aircraft and in November 1945 it moved to Chivenor. Docking closed early in 1946 and was finally sold in April 1958.

DOWNHAM MARKET

This station opened as a satellite to Marham from 1941 to September 1942, and from May to September 1942 it was also used by 1655 Conversion Unit. The first Pathfinder Force (PFF) squadron stationed at Downham was 218 (Gold Coast) Squadron, which arrived in July 1942 and remained until March 1944, flying Stirling Is and IIIs. Harry Barker was the bomb aimer in Flying Officer John Overton's crew, which arrived at Downham Market in May 1943.

The airfield was close to the tiny village of Bexwell and our billets were dispersed among the fields away from the field. The officers' mess was the rectory and all other ranks lived in Nissen huts with a large building for our mess hall. We all found the place quite pleasant even if the new construction was obviously only partly completed. The fact that the weather was warm and everywhere seemed bright and green helped us to settle in. We soon borrowed old bikes and most evenings set off to explore the local villages for suitable pubs and places of interest. On 29 May we were briefed for an attack on Wuppertal in the Ruhr. The raid was at times a bit scary; we saw flak and searchlights for the first time and our trip lasted 4 hours 25 minutes. I remember the rewarding breakfast we had on return of bacon and egg and then getting back to our billet for six or

Stirling III BF480 *I-Ink* of 218 Gold Coast Squadron lies wrecked at Downham Market following the crew's disastrous operation to Bochum on 13/14 May 1943. *I-Ink* ploughed into a truck killing two airmen who had disembarked from Stirling BF413/T and were about to enter the operations block for interrogation. BF480 was damaged beyond repair. (*Arthur R. 'Spud' Taylor*)

seven hours' sleep. When I awoke and had my lunch in the sergeants' mess, I wandered off on my own and lay down on the warm turf outside our hut. It was beautiful day, a bright blue sky and birds were singing. I reflected on the incredible situation I was in. I was a very immature kid at twenty years old stretched out on warm Norfolk turf having very recently flown as a crew member of a huge bomber to drop bombs on a German town. Then I had helped to fly back to my well-earned bacon and egg before getting ready to do the same thing again. It all seemed so unreal. The routine on the squadron continued much the same; we had to carry out air tests and ground maintenance on our guns and turrets, cleaning the perspex and stripping down the guns, cleaning and oiling them. The perspex used to get covered with squashed insects, which had to be removed to avoid visibility problems in the air, which of course are much worse at night. A clean turret could save your life.

We tended to relieve any boredom from the flying duties by some fairly heavy drinking sessions at the local pubs. I

Acting Squadron Leader Ian Willoughby Bazalgette DFC RAFVR (seated, far left, second row) of 635 Squadron stationed at Downham Market, who was awarded a posthumous VC for gallantry displayed on 4 August 1944 during a daylight raid on the V-1 storage depot at Trossy St Maxim. (*via Tom Cushing*)

regret to say that the journeys home by bike were sometimes more hair-raising than the ops. I frequently pranged and my bike, which cost me 5 guineas at Bennetts in Downham Market, suffered grievously. One handlebar broke off and I was forced to get used to riding a single-sided machine thereafter, which was even more difficult to control at the end of a heavy session of 'black and tans' – our favourite drink. John Overton encouraged us to socialize and test all the local pubs. This was the norm for crews and helped form the vital bond that was essential for men working together and knowing that each man could depend on the others totally. We usually went out as a party of four or five and soon found that the Carpenter's Arms in Denver was most welcoming and hospitable. We could settle down for pints and a singsong until closing time. It had a fairly large room with a bar at one end and a piano at the other but best of all, there were a couple of pleasant young female members of the family who were accomplished pianists. The 'Chippies' soon became one of our favourite 'targets for tonight" when we were not flying. In fact our ground crew had already sorted it out as the nearest home from home and we often found quite a large assembly from the squadron ordering pints at the bar. After a few weeks of regular attendance at the 'Chippies', the landlord George Tingey and his wife Grace invited two or three of us in turn to share their Sunday dinner with them. Bearing in mind that this was during stringent civilian rationing, sharing their excellent roast beef and Yorkshire pudding was extremely generous!

On Saturdays there was a dance in the Denver village hall and this was popular with those of us who had consumed sufficient beer. I had found that Molly, the youngest granddaughter at the pub, was friendly and very attractive. She played the piano and the accordion and was therefore very popular and I found her company more and more desirable so visits to Denver were organized whenever possible, which provoked considerable ribbing from the rest of the crew. When I received my commission I had to move into the officers' mess, which at that time was the Old Rectory. We had to get used to the apparently smoother way of life; we had a batman to clean our buttons and shoes, to *make our beds and look after our clothes – it seemed as if we were living in another world! And on top of all this, all non-commissioned ranks had to salute us and call us 'sir'...We did tend to 'let ourselves go' when off duty. We drank a great deal of beer and used any excuse for a party commonly described as a 'piss-up' either in the mess or at a local pub. We got to know the locals, who were always friendly and understanding. Some shared their Sunday dinners with us and of course there were the girls ... Life on the squadron was a mixture of fun, laughter, friendships, excitement and hell, just around the corner. In the officers' mess we had a very good standard of living. The food was very good. Sleeping quarters were comfortable and we had either a batwoman or batman to look after us, cleaning shoes, brass buttons etc and pressing uniforms and making beds. I usually had a cup of tea brought to me in bed every morning! At the end of our stay, the squadron was moved to Woolfox Lodge near Stamford, which was our new home for the next seven months. I was very sorry to leave Downham and the friends we had all made there but this was what service life is like and it was pointless to moan.*

On 10 August 1943 623 Squadron was formed from a flight of 218 Squadron with Stirling IIIs but it was short-lived and disbanded on 6 December, by which time the squadron had flown 150 sorties. Two aircrew members were posthumously awarded the VC while serving at Downham Market. The first was to Flight Sergeant Arthur Louis Aaron DFM, pilot of a 218 Stirling, won for the most conspicuous bravery during operations on the night of 12 August 1943 while making an attack on the Fiat works at Turin. Over the target his Stirling was hit by machine-gun fire from the rear gunner of another Stirling. Aaron was seriously injured and although his aircraft was badly damaged in the cockpit, turrets and engines, he helped his crew fly the aircraft for another five hours until they crash-landed at Bone airfield in North Africa.

No.214 Squadron, equipped with Stirlings, arrived in December but left in January 1944 for Sculthorpe where it became part of 100 Group. On 20 March 'B' Flight of 35 Squadron and 'C' Flight of 97 Squadron joined forces to form 635 Squadron, which was equipped with Lancaster Is and IIIs for pathfinding duties. During the latter half of 1944 it had about

Airmen at Downham Market found the Carpenter's Arms in Denver 'a most welcoming and hospitable' pub and the 'Chippies' soon became one of the aircrews' favourite 'targets for tonight' when they were not flying. It is now a private residence. (*Author*)

five Lancaster IVs on strength. The second award of the VC to an airman at Downham Market was to Acting Squadron Leader Ian Willoughby Bazalgette DFC RAFVR of 635 Squadron, who was master bomber, for his gallantry during the daylight attack on a V-1 storage depot at Trossy St Maxim on 4 August. Bazalgette's Lancaster (ND811 F2-T) was badly hit by flak just short of the target and both starboard engines were put out of action, the wing and fuselage set on fire and the bomb aimer seriously wounded. Bazalgette however pressed on to the target while the crew tried to douse the fire and he dropped his markers. With only one engine still running and the starboard wing a mass of flame the order to bale out was given. The bomb aimer was incapacitated and the mid-upper gunner had been overcome by fumes and were unable to bale out so Bazalgette put the aircraft down in a field but the Lancaster exploded, killing all three on board. When the surviving crew returned to the UK they told the story and Bazalgette was awarded a posthumous VC on 17 August 1945.

No.571 Squadron had formed at Downham on 7 April 1944

The Old Rectory adjacent to Bexwell Church once served as the officers' mess for aircrews from Downham Market. Inside the church is a memorial tablet to squadrons that operated from the airfield and the VC memorial in the churchyard includes detailed inscriptions of the two actions concerning Flight Sergeant Arthur Louis Aaron DFM, and Acting Squadron Leader Ian Willoughby Bazalgette DFC RAFVR. (*Author*)

as a light-bomber unit of 8 (Pathfinder) Group equipped with Mosquito VIs, moving to Oakington later the same month. On 1 August 608 Squadron was formed at Downham as part of 8 (Pathfinder) Group's Light Night Striking Force with Mosquito XXs, flying more than 1,700 sorties, mainly against industrial targets, until it disbanded on 24 August 1945. No.635 Squadron disbanded on 1 September 1945. The station then came under the control of 42 Group and became a satellite of 274 MU, with a number of Mosquitoes being stored for a few months. All flying ended in April 1946 and the station closed on 24 October. The site was sold for civilian use in February 1957.

EAST WRETHAM

A large square grass meadow in Breckland south-west of East Wretham village was hastily developed as a satellite landing ground for RAF Honington's Wellingtons in the spring of 1940.

Properties nearby were requisitioned and Wretham Hall was taken over and used as an officers' mess. A few huts were erected but some personnel would have to live in tents until permanent accommodation became available on dispersed campsites north-west and north-east of the airfield where eight domestic and one communal site and sick quarters were built eventually. Two (later three) grass runways, the main 1,880 yards (with PSP laid in 1944) and two 1,400 yards long were laid. Over the next two years twenty-four Macadam hardstandings with long access tracks and twelve using PSP were constructed and a technical site erected on the western side with two Bellman hangars, six blisters and one steel frame and canvas hangar. From mid-1940 onwards squadrons from Honington were rotated to East Wretham and on 16 September the ground echelon of 311 Czech Squadron that had begun operations in 3 Group on Wellingtons from Honington arrived.

No.311 was the first and only Czechoslovak squadron in Bomber Command, having been formed in July 1940 from airmen who had been serving in France. The squadron's Wellingtons arrived on 19 September but operations would still be flown from the parent aerodrome and that afternoon five Wimpys returned to Honington, though the night operation was later cancelled. The Czechs' first operation from East Wretham was flown on the night of 21/22 September, when the target was Calais. Landing back at East Wretham in the dark on a grass runway marked out with Glim flares proved difficult when fog descended and only Flight Lieutenant Ocelca landed, damaging his aircraft in the process. On 23/24 September three crews set out for Berlin, one returning early. The second reached the target but the third was forced to put down in Holland, where the crew escaped. On 16/17 December 1940 when three Wimpys set out for Mannheim, P2577/Q aborted and crashed on the Wretham–Wretham Hall road and burst into flames. Pilot Officer Nedved scrambled clear and, despite exploding bombs, returned to rescue his crew, one of whom was critically injured. Despite the seclusion of East Wretham during the winter of 1940/41 German intruders were often in evidence. On 3 February 1941 twenty bombs were dropped and thirteen fell on the landing ground, damaging a Wellington. On the night of 3/4 March a Ju 88C followed one of the Wellingtons into Wretham and dropped ten bombs before flying away. Near Upwood on 8/9 April *Leutnant*

Wellington Ic R1410 KX-M of 311 (Czechoslovakian) Squadron in March 1941. R1410 passed to 12 OTU where, on on the night of 25/26 June 1942 when the 1,000-bomber raid on Bremen took place, it crashed off the Friesians probably after being attacked by Major Kurt Holler of StII/NJG2. Eighteen-year old pilot Sergeant J. T. Shapcott and his crew were killed. That same night 311 Squadron were part of Coastal Command and stationed at Bircham Newton for the raid on Bremen. (*RAF Honington*)

Hans Hahn of III/NJG2 in a Ju 88C shot down 'X-X-ray', which was on a night-training flight. (The Czech Training Unit, which on 1 January 1942 became 1429 Operational Training Flight, also operated at Wretham with up to twelve Wellington Ics and three Airspeed Oxfords.)

No.311 Squadron operated from Norfolk and Suffolk until 1 May 1942, flying 145 operations and losing twenty aircraft. The Czechs then left for Aldergrove in Northern Ireland, having been transferred to RAF Coastal Command. No.311 Squadron flew Liberators on long-range maritime operations until the end of the war. During May and June 1429 Flight took part in the three 1,000-Bomber raids, six Wellingtons being flown on the Cologne raid on 30/31 May and again on 1/2 June (Essen) and 25/26 June

(Bremen). (*see also Bircham Newton*). The flight moved to Woolfox Lodge on 1 July and in August East Wretham was placed under 'care and maintenance' as plans had been formulated to develop the site as a Class A bomber station. However, work was delayed when runway construction at Mildenhall resulted in 115 Squadron's Wellington IIIs being moved to East Wretham on 21 November for a temporary stay; East Wretham became Mildenhall's third satellite. No.115 Squadron's final Wellington III sorties were flown from Wretham on 12 March 1943 and the squadron converted to the Hercules radial-powered Lancaster II.

A detached flight of 1657 Conversion Unit (CU) formed on 22 March using eight Lancaster IIs for crew conversion (In May it became 1678 CU). The first Lancaster operation from East Wretham was flown on 20/21 March when four aircraft laid mines off the Biscay ports. On 22/23 March 115 Squadron was part of the force that attacked St Nazaire, and its first major raid on Berlin was on 27/28 March. Thereafter 115 Squadron was fully committed to Main Force operations.

Meanwhile, on 24 March 1943, 32 Base HQ opened at Mildenhall and administered East Wretham until 7 August. The aerodrome never was developed into a Class A standard airfield because in June it was reallocated to the US Eighth Air Force for fighter use. No.115 Squadron and 1678 CU and their Lancasters left for Little Snoring in August, as there were no other suitable stations available in the 3 Group area of Suffolk and Cambridgeshire. During RAF Bomber Command operations from East Wretham sixty aircraft were lost, thirty-nine of them Wellingtons (nineteen from 311 Squadron on 152 operations) and twenty-one Lancasters.

East Wretham was officially transferred to the Eighth Air Force in September 1943 with accommodation for 190 officers and 1,519 enlisted men. The P-47D Thunderbolt-equipped 359th Fighter Group with its three squadrons arrived in October. This group made its combat debut on 13 December, converting to P-51 Mustangs the following spring and remaining at the Norfolk base until 10 November 1945, when the 359th Fighter Group was deactivated, the base having officially returned to 12 Group, RAF Fighter Command on the 1st. On 23 February 1946 Fighter Command decided that they no longer needed East Wretham and on 21 May the Air Ministry transferred it to 1 Group Bomber

Command. On 10 July it passed to RAF Technical Training Command and the camp was later used to house Polish veterans and their families. Some parts of East Wretham were sold off in October 1954, although the British Army retained several of the campsites for use and much later incorporated a large part of the airfield into the Stanford Training Area. A Bellman hangar and some wartime buildings remain in use for various purposes.

FELTWELL

A 280-acre landing field was created at Feltwell in 1917 to accommodate a training depot station (the old hospital buildings could still be seen on the south-east side of the present airfield as late as 1984), and a tramway was laid from Lakenheath railway station. (The track was later taken up and sent to Australia.) On 7 May 1919 a sale by tender took place and by March 1920 the site had closed.

Feltwell was re-established as part of the 1930s expansion programme and it reopened on 12 March 1937 in 3 Group, Bomber Command. On 16 April 1937 Handley Page Harrows of 214 Squadron arrived from Scampton and ten days later 37 Squadron was re-formed from 'B' Flight of 214 Squadron. The Harrow was originally designed as a transport but entered service as a bomber, powered by two Bristol Pegasus piston engines giving a top speed of about 200 mph.

On 29 April 1937 two Harrows of 214 Squadron collided and crashed near Wissington sugar factory. In May 1939 both squadrons began re-equipment with Vickers Wellington I bombers. In June 1939 the Harrows left 37 Squadron. In September 214 Squadron, by now flying Wellington IC aircraft, moved to the satellite airfield at Methwold, where Wellingtons of 37 Squadron had dispersed. Early 3 Group Wellington operations, unescorted and in broad daylight, proved suicidal in the face of German fighter and flak defences. (On 14 December five out of twelve Wellingtons were shot down.) But a second large Wellington raid went ahead on Monday 18 December to attack enemy shipping off Wilhelmshaven. Six Wellingtons of 37 Squadron formed part of the force of twenty-four Wellingtons of 9, 37 and 149 Squadron, which raided warships at Heligoland. Flying Officer 'Cheese' Lemon of 37 Squadron went to dump his bombs but instead of opening the bomb doors he lowered his

Feltwell's Second World War era hangars and other original buildings, long since converted for USAF use, photographed from the nose of Lancaster BI PA474 of the BBMF in September 1999. (*Author*)

flaps with a resulting gain of considerable height. Enemy fighters missed his aircraft but shot down the other five. Altogether, twelve of the twenty-two attacking Wellingtons were shot down. Lemon crash-landed at Feltwell and the Wellington was destroyed.

In late 1939 the New Zealand Flight moved to Feltwell as part of 3 Group, also flying Wellingtons. This Flight was attached to 75 Squadron, which at the time was the 3 Group Pool Squadron; being non-operational, it was used for training the Wellington crews of the group. In April 1940 75 Squadron was merged with 148 Squadron to form 15 OW at Harwell. The flight remained at Feltwell, becoming 75 Squadron RNZAF – the first Commonwealth squadron to form. On the night of 17/18 April 75 Squadron despatched three Wellingtons to Stavanger, the *Luftwaffe* having established a large supply base for their Norwegian campaign. (Three Wellingtons had been despatched from Feltwell on 4 April but had been recalled.) Two aircraft bombed the target. Thereafter, the Wellingtons were employed on North Sea sweeps and night-reconnaissance operations over the island of Sylt to prevent mine-laying seaplanes from operating. In

An aerial view of Feltwell showing the 'golf balls' of the US Space Command's 5th Space Surveillance Squadron, which house surveillance equipment. (*Author*)

the afternoon of 24 September, a stick of fourteen bombs fell on Feltwell, hitting an ammunition dump, damaging a hangar and wrecking Wellington Ic L7790 of 37 Squadron. No.57 Squadron arrived at Feltwell on 18 November 1940 with Wellington Ic and II aircraft.

On the night of 7/8 July 1941 Wellingtons of 75 Squadron raided Munster. On the return flight at 13,000 feet over Ijsselmeer, Squadron Leader R. P. Widdowson's aircraft (L7818) was attacked by a Bf 110 night fighter. The rear gunner was wounded in the foot but managed to drive off the enemy aircraft. Incendiary shells from the fighter started a fire near the starboard engine which fed by a fractured fuel pipe, soon threatened to engulf the whole wing. Sergeant James Ward RNZAF, the second pilot, climbed out of the astrodome into a 100-mph slipstream in pitch darkness a mile above the North Sea. By kicking holes in the fabric covering of the geodetics, he inched his way to the starboard engine and smothered the fire, which threatened to engulf the aircraft, which landed safely at Newmarket. Ward's actions earned him the VC. (He was killed two months later in a Wellington over Hamburg.)

No.1519 Beam Approach Training Flight was formed at Feltwell in December 1941 with Oxford I trainers. In January 1942 57 Squadron moved to Methwold, with 75 Squadron RNZAF moving to Mildenhall in August 1942; the same month that Feltwell was transferred to 2 Group, Bomber Command. On 15 August 1942 487 Squadron RNZAF, followed a month later by 464 Squadron RAAF, formed at Feltwell with Ventura light bombers and with 21 Squadron at Methwold similarly equipped, made up the Ventura wing.

On 6 December 1942 forty-seven Venturas, including fourteen of 464 RNZAF and sixteen of 487 RAAF Squadron took part in Operation Oyster, a daylight attack on the Philips factories at Eindhoven by ninety-three light bombers. Fourteen aircraft (including nine Venturas) failed to return.

In April 1943 the Australian and New Zealand squadrons moved to Methwold and Feltwell went over to a bomber-support role with the arrival of 192 Squadron, initially with Wellingtons and Mosquitoes for the RCM role. Some Halifax aircraft also joined the unit. About the same time the Bomber Development Unit (BDU) arrived from Gransden Lodge with Manchester, Halifax, Lancaster and later, Mosquito aircraft. During this period 20 Glider Maintenance Section was responsible for storing about thirty Horsas at Feltwell and Methwold. Feltwell returned to 3 Group control in July 1943 and in September 1473 (RCM) Flight arrived with Wellingtons while the BDU moved to Newmarket. On 25 November 192 Squadron left for Foulsham, where it was soon joined by 1473 Flight. Feltwell became 3 Group Lancaster Finishing School (LFS) on 19 December 1943 with four Lancasters. Two Lancasters collided near the aerodrome and crashed at Hockwold on 18 December 1944. The G-H Training Flight of 3 Group formed at Feltwell on 29 December with 8 Lancaster I/III aircraft with FN.121 turrets and G-H radar equipment and disbanded in June 1945. On 31 January 1945 3 LFS was disbanded and the BDU returned, joined on 26 February by 1688 Bomber Defence Training Flight. In January 1946 the BDU left for Marham, where it was integrated with the Central Bomber Establishment. No.1688 BBDTF left for Wyton on 19 March 1946.

Feltwell was transferred to Flying Training Command and 3 Flying Training School (FTS) occupied the airfield from April 1946 to April 1958 with a variety of training aircraft. No.77

Squadron re-formed at Feltwell in August 1958 as the first Thor IRBM unit, which became the main training station for the Thor detachments stationed at Shepherds Grove (82 Squadron), Tuddenham (107 Squadron) North Pickenham (220 Squadron) and Mepal (113 Squadron). Each squadron was equipped with three missiles. The Thors were phased out in 1963 and 77 Squadron disbanded on 15 August 1963. The airfield was reopened for use by communications aircraft until on 30 September 1965 MoD announced that Feltwell would be run down and closed by December 1966. The USAF took over the station in 1967 and used it mainly for accommodation purposes for Mildenhall personnel and later by the 48th TFW of Lakenheath as a storage base and for living accommodation.

FERSFIELD

This airfield was built in 1943 and it opened in July 1944 as a standard bomber station with a 2,000-yard main runway, two 1,400-yard runways and two T2 hangars. Accommodation was constructed to house 421 officers and 2,473 other ranks. During 1944 the remoteness of this base was used to great effect by units involved in two top secret projects known as Aphrodite (USAAF) and Anvil (US Navy). These detachments used war-weary Flying Fortresses and PB4Y-1 Liberator bombers respectively, loaded with up to 20,000 pounds of HE and used as remotely controlled

Fersfield airfield photographed in July 1999. (*Author*)

BBMF Spitfire XIX PS915 photographed from the rear turret of Lancaster BI PA474 with Fersfield airfield in the background on Battle of Britain Day, 15 September 1999. The RAF's Historic Aircraft Flight operated from Horsham St Faith from November 1961 to April 1963, when it moved to RAF Coltishall, becoming the BBMF in 1973 and leaving for Coningsby in March 1976. In September 1957 PS915 was grounded until 1986. (*Author*)

flying bombs. A crew of two would fly the 'drone' as it was called, to the east coast, where they would bale out and it then came under radio control from a mother aircraft, which would remotely steer it to its target (underground V-weapons storage sites and the like). On 12 August 1944 Lieutenant Joe Kennedy USN (brother of the future President Kennedy) and his co-pilot were killed when their PB4Y-1 exploded near Blythburgh. Twenty missions were flown but none proved successful before the project was abandoned in late 1944. Fersfield was returned to the RAF and in mid-December, 2 Group of 2nd Tactical Air Force moved its Group Support Unit (GSU) into the station, which became a holding camp for replacement aircrews. No.2 GSU B-25 Mitchells flew a few operations.

Early in 1945 Fersfield was the start of one of the most

memorable RAF operations of the Second World War. Special Operations Executive (SOE) in London had received intelligence that various Resistance and political prisoners held captive in the *Gestapo* HQ Shellhaus building in Copenhagen were to be shot on 21 March. Eighteen Mosquito crews of 21 Squadron, 464 Squadron RAAF and 487 Squadron RNZAF in 140 Wing at Thorney Island were therefore despatched to Fersfield to plan a daring pinpoint raid on the Shellhaus on the 20th. (Fersfield, 350 miles from the target, was chosen to minimize the risks of flying over enemy territory.) The Mosquitoes, each loaded with eleven-second delayed-action bombs rendezvoused over the North Sea with Mustang IIIs of 64 and 126 Squadrons from Fersfield. The raid cost four Mosquitoes and two of the Mustang escorts but the Shellhaus was well hit and thirty Danish hostages, including two Resistance leaders, escaped but some bombs hit the Jeanne D'Arc School in error and destroyed it, killing eighty-six of the 482 children.

No.41 RSU, which collected 2 Group's crashed aircraft for salvage and repair, arrived in 1945 and remained until 30 April. In June Mitchells of 180 Squadron and in July, Mosquito FBVIs of 605, 140 and 613 'City of Manchester' Squadrons arrived for armament training conducted by 2 Group Training Flight. On 1 August 2 Group Disbandment Centre was formed to supervise the winding down of 2 Group squadrons before Fersfield passed to 12 Group, Fighter Command, on 31 December. On 23 February 1946 Fersfield passed to the Air Ministry and the airfield was put up for disposal, being rapidly returned to agriculture.

FOULSHAM

Construction of Foulsham airfield 15 miles north-west of Norwich in the parishes of Wood Norton and Foulsham and ½ mile north of the village of the same name began in 1941 and was almost complete by the late summer of 1942. Three concrete runways, the main of 1,900 yards, one of 1,400 yards and one of 1,350 yards, a perimeter track and thirty-sevem hardstandings of the pan type, two hangars, a control tower and associated buildings built mainly by Kirk & Kirk Ltd were erected. Domestic sites for 2,135 airmen and 355 WAAFs were dispersed in farmland south of the Skitfield road to the east of the airfield and

Mitchell IIs of 180 Squadron from Foulsham in May 1943. This airfield became the operational station for 98 and 180 Squadrons, equipped with the North American Mitchell in October 1942 but these two squadrons did not fly their first operation until 23 January 1943. In mid-August the Mitchell squadrons moved to Dunsfold in Surrey. No.180 Squadron returned briefly to Norfolk in April 1944 when it was at Swanton Morley and again in 1945 when it was stationed at Fersfield during July. (*John Smith-Carrington via Theo Boiten*)

the bomb dump was off the south-west side. Eventually seven hangars – six T2s and a B1 – were erected on the main technical area on the east side of the airfield. Another T2 was built on the south-west side near Wades Farm and two more T2s on the south-east corner by Millhill Farm. (Five of the hangars were built during 1943–44 for use by 12 MU for assembling and storing Horsa gliders.)

In May 1942 the airfield was allocated to 2 Group, Bomber Command, and in October it became the operational station for 98 and 180 Squadrons equipped with the North American Mitchell. These two squadrons did not fly their first operation until 23 January 1943, when six of 98 Squadron, led by Wing Commander Lewer and six of 180 Squadron, led by Wing Commander C. C. Hodder AFC attacked the Perfine oil tanks and the Sinclair oil refinery by the Ghent-Terneuzen canal in Belgium. The raid went ahead twenty-four hours late because the necessary bombs were not forthcoming on the 21st. Flying at wave-top height all the way, an unlikely hazard was encountered by

Squadron Leader Slocombe, in a 98 Squadron Mitchell, who was injured in the face when a seagull shattered his canopy. He had to abort the operation. Bombing was made from 1,500 feet amid heavy flak and fighter attack, which were responsible for the loss of a 98 Squadron Mitchell and two 180 Squadron aircraft, one of them flown by Wing Commander Hodder. Sergeant T. S. Martin's Mitchell of 180 Squadron endured six attacks by Fw 190s before Mustang Is of 169 Squadron drove off the German fighters, though two Mustangs were shot down.

On 11 May the Mitchells of 180 Squadron resumed operations when railway communications at Boulogne were the target of six aircraft but bad weather prevented bombing and one aircraft was lost. Next day Mitchells of 98 Squadron bombed the target successfully. On 15 and 16 May 98 Squadron bombed Caen airfield and 180 Squadron flew their first Circus operation on the 16th when Triqueville was attacked. No.2 Group transferred to the 2nd Tactical Air Force on 1 June 1943 and in mid-August the Mitchell squadrons moved to Dunsfold in Surrey. Foulsham passed to 3 Group on 1 September 1943 when 514 Squadron arrived with radial-engined Lancaster B.II bombers and two weeks later 1678 Heavy Conversion Unit arrived from Little Snoring to train the crews of 514 Squadron. The first operational raid by 514 Squadron was on the night of 2/3 November, when two aircraft were despatched to Düsseldorf and four laid mines near the Friesian Isles. On 23 November both units moved to Waterbeach after only six operations to make way for 100 Group tenure.

No.180 Squadron Mitchell IIs at Foulsham in June 1943. The nearest aircraft is FL684/S, which operated with the squadron from 19 June until 20 March 1944. Behind is FL707/Z, which served with the squadron from 3 October 1942 and was shot down on 26 November 1943 during a raid on Martinvast. (*John Smith-Covington via Theo Boiten*)

GREAT MASSINGHAM

This airfield, directly adjacent to Great Massingham village, was built in 1940 as a satellite for West Raynham 2 miles away. In August Blenheims of 18 Squadron were the first to arrive from their parent station as Sergeant Jim 'Dinty' Moore, one of the Blenheim air gunners, recalls:

The squadron dispatched sixty-two aircraft on operations, losing four aircraft and their crews, none of whom we had the opportunity to really get to know. During the latter part of August we moved our squadron's aircraft to a temporary aerodrome at Great Massingham to spread our aircraft to minimize the damage that could be caused by attacks from enemy bombers. Apart from the landing field, there were none of the buildings one found on a permanent 'drome, only a few Nissen huts. It was necessary therefore to find accommodation for us in the lovely little villages of Great Massingham and Little Massingham, which adjoined the airfield. They were so close, in fact, that the roofs of one row of cottages were damaged from time to time by the trailing aerials of Blenheims when the WOp/AG had forgotten to wind them in before coming in to land. Great Massingham was built around two large ponds and a village green and had two or three public houses [including the Fox and Pheasant, otherwise known as the Poxy Pheasant]. The problem of accommodation was solved by literally taking over both villages, the sergeants' mess being housed in a rather dismal, rambling old rectory [now demolished] in Little Massingham. Another building was taken over as a theatre, dance hall or church as required, another as our operations room and so on. On 9 September leaving 101 Squadron to the delights of West Raynham, all air and ground crews followed our aircraft and moved into whatever accommodation had been found for us.

'Oh God!' was the first thought which entered the mind of 19-year-old Corporal Joe Beckett, an armourer. Joe was luckier than some, being billeted in the grounds of the Birkbeck estate not far from Little Massingham church. He found Lady Joan Birkbeck kindness itself and a friend to all, regardless of rank or status. Many found Great Massingham a friendly village.

Enemy tip-and-run raids in the area between May and October

Boston IIIs photographed at a press day at Great Massingham on 8 April 1942. The nearest aircraft is AL280/A, which was hit by flak at Vlissingen and ditched in the North Sea on 1 August 1942. (*Tony Carlisle via Nigel Buswell*)

1940 caused some damage, the worst on 27 October when an enemy aircraft dropped incendiaries, causing the first deaths to enemy action and destroying a Blenheim at Great Massingham. On the evening of 14 November 1940, as 437 *Luftwaffe* crews raided Coventry, thirty-five Blenheims of 18 Squadron and three other squadrons carried out intruder attacks on German aerodromes in northern France and Belgium to cause as much disruption as possible. All the Blenheims returned safely. During December operations were again curtailed by the weather. The targets, both airfields and industrial sites, were often blanketed by low cloud. Bad weather dogged operations in England throughout December and although operations were briefed every day only a handful of sorties were flown. On 3 April 1941 18 Squadron moved to Oulton and on 11 May 107 Squadron, commanded by Wing Commander Laurence V. E. Petley, arrived from Leuchars, Scotland, where they had been stationed since March, attached to Coastal Command flying shipping sorties. The main party arrived by train on the Midland and Great Northern Line (or the 'Muddle and Go Nowhere Line', as it was known) at East Rudham station, marching up to the main gate of West Raynham at 11 p.m. They were greeted by a German air raid, which damaged a hangar and killed some girls in the NAAFI. The last leg of the journey was a mile-long march up the hill to Little Massingham, where there would be the first sight of the airfield. No sooner had the Blenheim crews touched down and found their billets, in houses and country homes in the

No.18 Squadron in front of the Old Rectory at Massingham (now demolished) in March 1941. The squadron operated from Massingham from 8 September 1940 until 3 April 1941 (*Mrs Vera Sherring*)

village, than they were on their way again, this time on a shipping strike off Heligoland on 13 May. Twelve aircraft were detailed to attack and they flew across the North Sea in line abreast, led superbly by leading navigator Sergeant J. C. 'Polly' Wilson RNZAF. Two Blenheims returned early with mechanical problems, but the remaining aircraft went in at 200–400 feet and dropped almost four tons of bombs smack on the target. The attack was achieved with complete surprise and the Blenheims were safely away before the *Luftwaffe* could intervene.

On 15 May personnel of 90 Squadron arrived from a two-day sojourn at Bodney while their Fortress Is were flown to West Raynham for overhaul. Because of the poor runways and dispersals the Boeing boys in blue did most of their flying from West Raynham. By 26 May four crews had converted successfully to the Fortress and there were by then five aircraft on the squadron strength. Tom Imrie DFM, a WOp/AG and a veteran of thirty-four operations on Whitleys, noted that they 'moved about so much that they hardly ever had time to unpack, but morale always remained high. At West Raynham we shared the station with two Blenheim squadrons which at the time had suffered high losses in attacks on the Channel ports.' Peter B. Gunn, author of *RAF Great Massingham*, says that 'Kenneth Wolstenholme (the famous post-war football commentator) remembers one of the first Fortresses to arrive and the 107 Squadron crews "scampering all over it to have a look". The thing that impressed him at first were ashtrays that were provided but then it was a bit of a let-down to find out that these large aircraft did not carry many more bombs than the Mosquito!' At the end of August the squadron, which had still not yet flown a Fortress bombing operation, moved to Polebrook airfield in Northamptonshire.

On 7 June 1941 nine crews of 107 Squadron took part in a raid on a heavily defended convoy *en route* from Hamburg to Rotterdam. One of the pilots was Pilot Officer (later Squadron Leader) Bill Edrich, the famous England and Middlesex cricketer, who had joined the squadron on 31 May. (Another pilot who later served at Massingham was Keith Miller, the Australian all-rounder.) On 27 June ten crews from 107 Squadron flew to Swanton Morley for a special briefing where they and ten crews from 105 were told that they would carry out a low-level attack in daylight on the docks at Bremen the following day. When they reached a point opposite Cuxhaven they saw a large enemy

58

convoy, which opened up on them, so the essential element of surprise had been lost. Wing Commander Petley, who was leading, brought the formation home. Back at Massingham the crews went straight over to the cottage that housed their tiny operations room and HQ where a telephone call from the Air Officer Commanding (AOC), Air Chief Marshal Donald F. Stevenson DSO OBE MC, left the squadron in no doubt that he was not best pleased. The outcome was that they would have to make a return trip to Bremen and Operation *Wreckage* went ahead on 4 July. Petley led fifteen Blenheims of 107 Squadron, three returning early with mechanical problems. Petley was shot down by flak in the target area, killing him, his observer and his air gunner. Four crews in total were lost but successful attacks had been made on the docks, factories, a timber yard and railways and great damage was caused to the tankers and transports that were loaded with vital supplies. All the aircraft were damaged.

After *Wreckage* 107 Squadron needed to be re-formed before it could participate in further raids. At West Raynham, it took shape again. On 6 July Wing Commander Arthur F. Calvert Booth took command but within a week he was killed by flak during a shipping strike off Ijmuiden. On 12 August when fifty-six Blenheims attacked two power stations at Cologne 107 Squadron crews were part of Force 2. In all twelve Blenheims were lost. The mood among the crews was determined but at the same time it could be grim. Flying Officer Ewels recalled the

The religious retreat, which in the Second World War was used as a mess by RAF units at Massingham. (*Author*)

atmosphere. 'One evening after a hazardous operation the wing commander and other pilots in the mess at Little Massingham Manor sat for a long time in silence and then quietly got out notepaper and wrote out their wills. Not long afterwards all were gone.' Kenneth Wolstenholme (whose New Zealand navigator was killed beside him in a Blenheim on 21 May 1941) recalls:

> *You sometimes had to go to a funeral and on these occasions you were given a Union Jack to take to the undertaker but you also had to bring it back, and some undertakers could do it very nicely but others would go up to the coffin during the service and snatch it off! The awful thing was that you could be invited back to the house and introduced as one of the 'comrades' of the dead man, at the same time carrying the wretched flag wrapped up in brown paper. Actually we didn't do a lot of that – they didn't usually use aircrew, but if you were sick you sometimes had to go!*

To Wolstenholme Great Massingham seemed 'a bit primitive', with its rough grass field. Like other pilots he found the Blenheim a sturdy aircraft but 'it did not go at the speed all the aircraft recognition books said it did and at best 180 m.p.h. downhill and flat out'. There were few navigational aids – the R/T was local and there was no VHF. 'Dead reckoning' navigation was all there was, with a few radio fixes. What they did have were few in number and any aircraft losses were keenly felt. Everyone was waiting for the new American aircraft, the Bostons. Flying on Blenheims continued until the first Boston IIIs arrived at Massingham on 5 January 1942, while in Malta what was left of the detachment remained on the island until the 12th. The new role for 107 Squadron was to be high-level, pinpoint bombing with a dozen or more aircraft. Training took time and 107 Squadron was not considered ready when Operation *Fuller* was mounted on 12 February in a vain attempt to prevent the 'Channel Dash' by the battle-cruisers *Scharnhorst*, *Gneisenau* and *Prinz Eugen*, which were heading from their French berths to Germany. When the first 2 Group Boston operation took place on 8 March 107 Squadron provided six crews for a Circus operation to the Abbeville marshalling yards. Six more Bostons, three each from 88 and 107 Squadrons attacked the Comines power station. Circus operations remained the order of the day and casualties

A weather-beaten hangar and a cobweb-ridden and rusty piece of agricultural machinery both of which continue to survive the ravages of harsh Norfolk winters, pictured in November 2005. (*Author*)

were heavy. In April 107 Squadron alone lost seven aircraft from seventy-eight sorties dispatched and eleven aircrew were killed. Crews took part in the Dieppe operation on 19 August when 107 Squadron carried out thirty-two sorties without loss but several aircraft were hit. Throughout September and October pairs of Bostons continued low-level attacks on power stations in northern France. In November 107 Squadron flew eleven sorties for the loss of four Bostons and sixteen aircrew killed – an almost 40 percent loss rate. On 6 December twelve Bostons of 107 Squadron were part of the 2 Group force that attacked the Strijp Group main works of the Philips electrical factories in Eindhoven.

For most of spring 1943 107 Squadron had a 'rest' from operations and there was an intensive training programme consisting of close-formation flying, bombing and air-to-ground firing. By May 1943 107 was the only squadron still using Bostons on Circus operations. Re-equipment was slow and it was not until 1 February 1944 that 107 Squadron moved to Lasham near Alton in Hampshire that the Bostons were replaced with the Mosquito FBVI. In operations from Massingham, eleven Blenheims and twenty-six Bostons failed to return from 100 raids. In July 1943 342 'Lorraine' Squadron arrived with its Bostons from Sculthorpe but stayed only a few weeks before moving to

Hartford Bridge to join 107 Squadron there. 'Dinty' Moore remembers 342 Squadron: 'They were a lively crowd, easily identified by their navy blue uniforms. They had one fault, which was when they were airborne they would persist in using their radios to chatter to one another despite repeated warnings to comply with radio discipline. They could also boast the only female intelligence officer in the Air Force, the attractive Section Officer Massias.'

During September 1943 Great Massingham was closed for the building of concrete runways and extension. The completion of this work by the following April heralded a new phase in the airfield's life. Four T2 hangars had been erected – two on the east side of the airfield north of the village, two on the north-east side and a single B1 hangar to the south-east. The Unit Construction Company Ltd arrived to lay three runways and extend the area of the airfield to the west. The main runway was 2,000 yards in length and the two cross runways were each 1,400 yards long. The runway and perimeter track construction programme left only sixteen pan hardstandings remaining so twenty loop types were laid to take the number to thirty-six. The accommodation and technical site north-west of the village eventually consisted of dispersed sites, two communal, two WAAF, five domestic and sick quarters. Total accommodation was for 1,778 airmen and 431 WAAFs. The station sick quarters opened on 1 May 1944 (until then West Raynham had been responsible for medical treatment), on 12 May the NAAFI, and on the 16th the officers' mess. The now complete airfield was allocated to 100 Group and 1694 Target Towing Flight (later known as Bomber Defence Training Flight) formed at Great Massingham and 1692 Bomber Support Training Flight arrived from Little Snoring with Beaufighters. On 4 June 169 Squadron flew in from Little Snoring to resume its bomber support role equipped with Mosquito night-fighters. (*see also West Raynham.*)

HORSHAM ST FAITH

Built before the war for use by RAF Bomber Command, Horsham St Faith was a grass airfield with five C-type hangars, permanent brick and tiled buildings with central heating and a high standard of domestic accommodation. With the outbreak of war it became necessary for the aerodrome to be used operationally, although construction work was still in progress. The first unit to use the station was a detachment of 21 Squadron flying Blenheim I and IVs during November and December 1939 while stationed at Watton. Various fighter squadrons were stationed at Horsham St Faith during daylight hours, 19 Squadron arriving during March 1940.

On 31 March Spitfire K9858 crashed on take-off. Its pilot was Flying Officer Douglas Bader, leading a flight of three Spitfires to intercept and identify a plot approaching a convoy. His Spitfire was in coarse pitch as all three tore across the grass. Seeing he could not lift off, the undercarriage was retracted and the Spitfire smashed through a low wall and ploughed across a field. Bader suffered a bump on the head and a dented leg. He took off in another Spitfire and rejoined his flight, circling the convoy for 1½ hours. No contact was made and they returned to Duxford. On 11 May 1940 three Spitfires of 19 Squadron shot down a Ju 88.

In early May 66 Squadron arrived with Spitfire Is and both units were engaged mainly on 'Kipper' and convoy patrols until late May when 19 left for Duxford and 66 for Coltishall. At this time detachments of Defiant Is of 264 Squadron were stationed at Horsham. With the departure of the fighters, the station was officially opened on 1 June 1940. No.114 Squadron arrived from Wattisham and 139 from West Raynham, both units flying Blenheim Ibs on offensive sweeps. No.114 Squadron left for Oulton in August and in February 1941 a detachment of 110 Squadron was stationed at St Faith with Blenheims. In the early

Bristol Blenheim IVs of 139 Squadron from Horsham St Faith taking off on a Circus operation in 1941. The squadron was stationed at the airfield from 10 June 1940 to 13 July 1941. (*Eric Atkins*)

Blenheim IV V550 intruder of 18 Squadron at Horsham St Faith in the winter of 1942. In March of that year 82, 139 and 110 Squadrons were dispatched to the Far East. The remaining Blenheims of 18, 21 and 114 Squadrons were used on night intruder operations against enemy airfields, which were to last until the final Blenheim of 18 Squadron landed at Wattisham on 18 August 1942.
(*Alan Ellender via Theo Boiten*)

afternoon of 14 November, as 437 *Luftwaffe* crews prepared to raid Coventry, 18 Squadron at Great Massingham, 105 Squadron using Wattisham as their advance base, 101 Squadron at West Raynham and 110 at Horsham St Faith were briefed for a counter-operation called *Cold Water*. Plans of the large-scale attack on Coventry were known in advance because of *Ultra* intelligence but the knowledge had to be kept secret from the Germans so no additional measures were taken to repel the raid. However, squadrons from 2 Group were directed to attack aerodromes from which the enemy bombers were operating to cause as much disruption as possible, and the heavies would simultaneously retaliate against a German town. That night as the *Luftwaffe* devastated the city centre of Coventry, killing 380 people and injuring 800 seriously, thirty-five Blenheims bombed airfields in northern France and Belgium. All returned safely.

On 4 April 1941 8 Beam Approach Training Flight arrived from Ipswich airport with Blenheims and by October had begun re-equipping with Oxford TIs. During May and June detachments of 139 Squadron were flown to Malta and in July the rest of the squadron moved to Oulton. Blenheim IVs of 18 Squadron replaced them, although on occasion crews were sent to Manston for Channel Stop operations. While there, on 19 August, a Circus was flown to St Omer airfield, during which Blenheim IV R3843/F dropped a crate on the airfield containing a spare pair of artificial legs for Wing Commander Douglas Bader, who was a PoW. In October 139 Squadron returned with Blenheims and then in December 139 and 18 Squadrons left for Oulton and Wattisham respectively.

Swanton Morley's grass airfield and unfinished state was proving unsuitable for 105 Squadron flying Blenheim IVs and Mosquito BIVs and so, in early December 1941 105 moved to Horsham St Faith. Mosquito spares at this time were non-existent, although the squadron was expected to become fully operational with sixteen to eighteen crews and a dozen aircraft within a six-month period. Only eight Mosquitoes had arrived by mid-May 1942 but 2 Group was anxious to despatch its new wonder aircraft as soon as possible. On 27 May 105 Squadron prepared four Mosquitoes with bombs and cameras to harass and obtain photographic evidence in the wake of the '1,000-bomber' raid on Cologne which went ahead on the night of 30/31 May.

On 8 June 139 Squadron was formed at Horsham St Faith with crews and a few B.IVs of 105 Squadron. It flew its first Mosquito sorties on 25/26 June, a low-level raid on the airfield at Stade, near Wilhelmshaven and returned after dark just as bombers for the third in the series of '1,000-bomber' raids were taking off for

Norwich Airport is today a thriving regional airport with a valuable link to Schiphol in Holland and its international routes. The runway and perimeter track layout is a valuable legacy of the halcyon days when the airfield was RAF Horsham St Faith. (*Author*)

Bremen. Two of 105 Squadron's Mosquitoes flew reconnaissance over the city after the raid and four more went to reconnoitre other German cities to assess damage and bring back photographs. On 2 July the first joint attack by 105 and 139 Squadron Mosquitoes took place when four aircraft from 105 Squadron carried out a low-level attack on the submarine yards at Flensburg and two Mosquitoes in 139 Squadron also bombed from high level. Two Mosquitoes and their crews failed to return. On 11 July the Mosquitoes bombed Flensburg again, as a diversion for the heavies hitting Danzig. One Mosquito made it home with part of the fin blown away by flak, and another crashed, possibly as a result of flying too low.

During July the first twenty-nine *Siren Raids* were flown. These involved high-level dog-leg routes across Germany at night, and were designed to disrupt the war workers and their families and ensure that they lost at least two hours' sleep before their shifts the following day. In August 1942 Squadron Leader D. A. G. Parry DFC and his observer Flight Lieutenant Robson of 105 Squadron carried out a successful courier trip in an unarmed Mosquito to Stockholm, Sweden. (BOAC had sustained heavy losses in the Bay of Biscay and North Sea area and had suspended flights. Nine months later, BOAC received Mosquito airliners and flew the route regularly.)

On 13 September 105 and 139 Squadrons received orders to vacate Horsham St Faith by 28 September, as the Americans were due to arrive to base medium bombers there. On 19 September six crews in 105 Squadron attempted the first daylight Mosquito raid on Berlin. Only one succeeded in bombing the 'Big City'. Six days later four Mosquitoes of 105 Squadron led by Squadron Leader George Parry, and flying from Leuchars in Scotland, bombed the *Gestapo* HQ in Oslo, Norway. One Mosquito failed to return. At least four bombs entered the roof of the building. One had remained inside and failed to detonate and the three others crashed through the opposite wall before exploding. AOC RAF Bomber Command described the raid as a 'first class show'. On the night of 26 September listeners to the BBC Home Service heard that a new aircraft, the Mosquito, had been revealed officially for the first time by the RAF and that four had made a daring rooftop raid on Oslo. On 29 September 105 and 139 Squadrons moved to Marham with the Mosquito Conversion Unit and replaced 115 and 218 Squadrons of 3 Group. Horsham

St Faith was then transferred to the US 8th Air Force for the duration of the war.

First to arrive were B-26 Marauders and then P-47 Thunderbolt units, which used Horsham St Faith during 1943. The Thunderbolts left in July and the station closed while three runways were laid to take heavy bombers with concrete hardstandings and a perimeter track. Horsham St Faith was transferred to Fighter Command on 10 July 1945. Over the next twenty years, beginning In August 1945, when 54 and 307 (Polish) Squadron arrived, flying Mustang III and IV fighters and Mosquito NF.XXX night-fighters respectively, the station was home to many and myriad squadrons. These included the last of the piston-engined fighters such as the Spitfire, Mustang, de Havilland Hornet twin-engined single-seat fighter and the first jet fighters such as the Gloster Meteor and Hawker Hunter. The Battle of Britain Flight operated a Hurricane and Spitfires from 1960 until 1963, when the station was inactivated. On 24 March 1967 the local authority purchased Horsham St Faith and in 1969 Norwich Airport was born.

LANGHAM

Langham airfield, on the north Norfolk coast, was first use during 1940 as grass-covered emergency landing ground. In 1941 it became a satellite of Bircham Newton, Coastal Command, and became available as a dispersal site. On 1 January Hudson I T9287 of 206 Squadron was carrying out low-level flying nearby when it hit a barn and crashed, killing all eight on board. On 16 May 1941 the navigator of a Beaufighter damaged in combat with an He 111 parachuted out near Langham while the pilot crash-landed at Stiffkey. Langham airfield was also used day and night by Wellington aircraft from Bircham Newton, East Wretham, Swinderby and Newmarket for circuits and bumps on training flights. Strong cross-winds were a constant hazard to aircraft and caused the loss of two Wellingtons of 300 (Polish) Squadron on 23 March 1941 and a 511 (Czech) Squadron Wimpy on 25 May 1941 which burst into flames and killed four of the crew. Total RAF personnel at Langham now numbered about fifty billeted mainly in Langham Hall and administered by Bircham Newton.

On 6 December 1941 'K' and 'M' Flights of No.1 Anti-Aircraft

Ye Olde Erks Casino at Langham in the early 1970s. (*Author*)

Co-operation Unit (AACU) arrived from Bircham Newton with twelve Hawker Henley target tugs, two Tiger Moths and a Lysander. (Early in August 1942 four Defiant TT.I target tugs arrived to replace the remaining Henleys but during October 1942 more Henleys replaced these.) During July 1942 the airfield ceased to be a satellite of Bircham Newton and became an independent station. The same month six black-painted Swordfish aircraft of 819 Squadron FAA with a long-range fuel tank in the third crew member's position arrived from Machrihanish, Scotland, for special duties. Detachments of 2 Squadron (Mustangs) and 251 Squadron (Tomahawks) were stationed at Langham while engaged on army co-operation exercises. On 1 August 1942 280 Squadron with fourteen Anson Is (later supplemented by a few Hudsons) arrived to fly predominantly ASR patrols. It was decided to close Langham airfield for expansion and lay concrete runways and in October 1942 280 and 819 Squadrons moved to Bircham Newton. 'K' and 'M' Flights of 1 AACU disbanded early that same month to re-form at Bircham Newton as 1611 and 1612 Target Towing Flights respectively. Personnel from the RAF Regiment occupied the accommodation while reconstruction ensued.

During February 1944 Group Captain A. E. Clouston arrived at Langham to take command of 16 Group, Coastal Command, though building work was still in progress. In April 1944 the station reopened when a Beaufighter wing was formed with 455 (RAAF) and 489 (RNZAF) Squadrons flying Flakbeau and Torbeau variants. Their main targets were E- and R-boats, flak ships and supply ships off the Dutch and Belgian coasts. No.280

Squadron returned during September 1944 with Warwick ASR.Is, which carried the airborne lifeboat and other rescue equipment. On 30 October the squadron moved to Ellough (Beccles), Suffolk. The Beaufighter wing left in October 1944 and towards the end of the year a detachment of Barracudas of 827 Squadron FAA operated from Langham. From July 1944 a number of Wellington GR.XIII aircraft of 324 Squadron at Docking often flew from Langham, where the squadron had moved by November. At first the Wellingtons were in normal Coastal Command colour scheme but they were later repainted black overall. These were replaced by GR.XIVs, which had H2S radar and Leigh lights, although the lights were soon removed from the aircraft. Mainly they searched for and attacked E-boats off the Dutch coast and dropped flares to illuminate targets for the North Coates Beaufighter Strike Wing. Operating alongside 324 were 612 Squadron, also with Wellington GR.XIVs, which were in the normal white colour scheme. No.524 Squadron disbanded on 25 May 1945 followed by 612 Squadron on 9 July.

From October 1944 521 Squadron's Hudsons, Gladiators, Hurricanes and Fortresses were stationed at Langham with a few aircraft operating from Docking on daylight meteorological flights. During October and November 1945 521 Squadron moved to Chivenor and Brawdy, leaving their Hurricane flight to become 1402 (Met) Flight (which disbanded in May 1946). No.245 Squadron arrived in November 1945 with Beaufighter TF.X aircraft, staying until May 1946 when they moved to Thorney Island. No.280 Squadron also returned once more in November 1945 ,still flying Warwick Is, moving two months later to Thornaby. For a few weeks from January 1946 the Coastal Command Fighter Affiliation Unit was stationed at Langham.

The Royal Netherlands Air Force Technical Training School was housed at Langham from June 1946 until about September 1947 when it moved back home to Deelen. The school used a number of instructional airframes, including a Beaufighter TF.X and an Anson I. Langham then spent a period under care and maintenance before reopening in March 1952. Between March and June 1952 2 Civilian Anti-Aircraft Cooperation Unit (CAACU) arrived from Little Snoring and Cambridge and took over the target facilities role from the recently disbanded 34 Squadron at Horsham St Faith. No.2 CAACU, which worked with the Royal Navy, local RAF squadrons, radar stations and

The airfield in June 1997 with the turkey-rearing sheds that were built on the concrete areas, except for the north-east–south-west runway, in evidence. Other unused sections of concrete were broken up in 1985 for road construction. The control tower is amongst the Second World War era buildings that survive. (*Author*)

The rare dome-trainer that at various times was used for anti-shipping and as an astro trainer for night navigation was cosmetically restored in 1999. (*Author*)

Weybourne anti-aircraft camp, disbanded in 1958.

From October 1951 to July 1957 the 50th Radio Controlled Aircraft Detachment of the US Army with pilotless target drones was stationed at Langham. The drones were deployed to Weybourne Anti-Aircraft Camp from where they were launched by catapult and recovered by parachute. A US Army Skysweep Anti-aircraft Gun Training Regiment was also located on one of the campsites. In the late 1950s the airfield was also available as an emergency landing ground for Sculthorpe-stationed aircraft.

The main runway at Langham was resurfaced in spring 1953 but in 1959 the station was closed and in 1961 the Air Ministry disposed of it, the land reverting to agriculture.

LITTLE SNORING

This airfield, north of the A148 and east of the Little Snoring to Great Snoring road, was built within eleven months by Taylor Woodrow between September 1942 and July 1943 as a satellite to Foulsham. Three runways, the main at 2,000 yards and two cross

A Lancaster B.II of 115 Squadron, which was stationed at this remote Norfolk airfield from August to November 1943 under 3 Group control. On 8 December 1943 the station was taken over by 100 Group. (*via Tom Cushing*)

runways both 1,400 yards in length and thirty-six hardstandings of the looptype were built. Owing to the gradients of adjacent land, several of these were on a loop taxiway off the north side of the perimeter track. It was necessary to close a road from Thursford to Little Snoring when construction began as this crossed the site. Two T2 hangars were placed adjacent to the main technical site in the south and another two were erected on the north side. A single B1 hangar was situated off the south-east perimeter. Two of the T2s were for Horsa glider storage. The bomb dump was to the north of the airfield. The camp, dispersed around Little Snoring village towards the A148 road, consisted of eight domestic, two mess and one communal site for 1,807 airmen and 361 WAAFs. Though built originally for 2 Group, Little Snoring became operational in August 1943 in 3 Group with the arrival of 1678 Heavy Conversion (HC) Flight and a few Lancaster B.IIs and 115 Squadron from East Wretham (which was to become an American fighter base) with 21 Lancaster B.II bombers. The Lancaster B.II was powered by four Bristol Hercules engines in place of the more usual Merlins. No.1628 HC Flight moved on to Foulsham in September with 115 Squadron remaining until November, during which time its targets included Peenemünde and Nuremberg. In November 1943 115 moved to Witchford in Cambridgeshire having lost three Lancasters in operations from Little Snoring and on 8 December the station was taken over by 100 Group.

LUDHAM

The pressures placed on both RAF Coltishall and its satellite airfield at Matlaske were so great that on 19 November 1941 a second satellite airfield was created at Ludham, Norfolk's most easterly airfield. Its proximity to the sea made Ludham an ideal location for maritime support operations and in mid-November 152 squadron at Swanton Morley sent sections of Spitfires there for convoy escort duty and attacks on E-boats. Just after 0830 hours on 27 November Bristol Beaufort II AW248 of 217 Squadron at Thorney Island landed at Coltishall. The crew disembarked to brief the pilots of twelve Spitfires which had been detached to Coltishall to escort the Beauforts on a daylight anti-shipping raid off the Dutch coast. Six Spitfires of 152 Squadron at Ludham were to escort the Beauforts whilst a further six

The watch office, now a Grade II listed building, has been purchased by a KLM airline pilot whose intention is to turn it into a holiday home. (*Author*)

Spitfires of 19 Squadron would provide withdrawal support. At 0930 hours the Beaufort took off with its escorts. Two further Beauforts of 217 Squadron joined the formation over Coltishall. After a low-level flight over the North Sea the formation approached the Dutch coast where the Spitfires engaged some Bf 109s as the Beauforts attacked a cargo ship of about 1,201 tons with bombs. From this very successful strike only Beaufort AW248 sustained damage, landing with a feathered starboard propeller after being hit by anti-aircraft fire from the ship.

In December 1941 19 Squadron arrived from Matlaske with Spitfire IIAs for convoy escort and patrol and bomber escort on 2 Group 'Circus' operations but also to defend Norwich during enemy activity. In April 1942 19 Squadron left for Hutton Cranswick and Ludham welcomed the Spitfire Vs of 610 (County of Chester) Squadron, who assumed the same roles as their predecessors. An increase in *Luftwaffe* night-bomber activity resulted in nightly standby flights or 'fighter nights', as they were known. On the evening of 27 April 1942 Norwich was attacked by a sizeable force of *Luftwaffe* bombers. Fighter Command responded with thirty-two aircraft, including nine Beaufighters of

68 Squadron at Coltishall and ten Spitfires of 610 Squadron but only three aircraft (Mosquitoes of 157 Squadron at Castle Camps) were equipped with AI radar sets and the raiders bombed with impunity.

Squadron Leader 'Johnnie' Johnson began his second association with the Coltishall area in 1942 when he was posted to command 610 (County of Chester) Squadron at Ludham. Group Captain Ronnie Lees, the Station Commander, told Johnson that Max Aitken's 68 Squadron was equipped with Beaufighters at Coltishall and the Whirlwinds of 137 Squadron were at Matlaske. Johnson's squadron was flying convoy patrols, reconnoitring enemy shipping off the Dutch coast as well as carrying out a few sweeps with squadrons from 11 Group and many Rhubarbs. On arrival, Johnson found that his deputy was Dennis Crowley-Milling. 'The Crow' had joined the squadron soon after his escape from France the previous autumn. He also found 610 Squadron to be a cosmopolitan bunch of individuals from Canada, Australia, France, New Zealand, Belgium, Rhodesia and Norway. The Norwegian pilot often had to explain his heritage after being mistaken for a member of the *Luftwaffe* when he used to venture out on his bicycle around the broads in search of a pint of beer! Johnson made it quite clear to Lees that his ambition was to take the squadron back to 11 Group, hopefully to Biggin Hill, Kenley or North Weald, and that he also wanted to re-equip with the new Spitfire IX. He soon discovered, however, that his squadron was not going to 11 Group, nor was it re-equipping with Spitfire IXs but it would swap places with 167 Squadron at Castletown, near Thurso, in northern Scotland! Johnson challenged the decision all the way to the top though the C-in-C, Air-Chief Marshal Sir Sholto Douglas, advised that they would be back in 11 Group by the following spring. In October 1942 610 Squadron duly moved to Castletown and 167 Squadron arrived at Ludham. A high proportion of the pilots were Dutch and they were delighted to have an opportunity of flying sorties to the Dutch coast, although convoy patrols remained a high priority.

On 28 January 1943 HM King George VI and HM Queen Elizabeth visited Ludham, Matlaske, Neatishead and Coltishall. Enemy raids persisted over the area on a daily basis. On 30 May Observer Corps posts in and around Norwich were warned that a Ju 88 had been reported circling Ludham and there might be further enemy activity. (In 1943 Ludham airfield was also used as a practice bombing range. The local population took their RAF neighbours to their hearts despite an unfortunate incident when a local farmer narrowly avoided being hit when bombs destined for the Ludham range narrowly missed his car on the Potter Heigham road!)

No.195 Squadron, which flew Typhoons, replaced 167 Squadron at Ludham on 13 May 1943. On 6 July Wing Commander Alexander 'Ragbags' Rabagliati DFC*, Wing Leader at Coltishall, who had sixteen victories, led a flight of seven Typhoons on a shipping strike in EK273/JE-DT, the personal mount of Squadron Leader Don Taylor, CO of 195 Squadron. Sixty miles from home, Rabagliati reported mechanical trouble with his Napier Sabre engine. He was seen to be climbing with smoke streaming from the engine before descending and crashing into the sea. The other members of his flight circled the aircraft before being forced to fly home due to fuel shortage. They were all convinced their CO had scrambled clear, as they saw his dinghy floating near to the point of impact. They duly reported this to the Coltishall sector and a Walrus, escorted by six Spitfires of 118 Squadron, set off on a rescue mission. (Rabagliati's brother, Flight Lieutenant Francis 'Rags' Rabagliati, an ex-Coastal Command Blenheim fighter pilot who had been wounded in a fight with Bf 110s, was on 278 ASR Squadron at Coltishall and he monitored the rescue effort.) By the time the Walrus and the Spitfire escort reached the search area, weather conditions were squally rain showers, thunderstorms and high seas. Nothing was found of the Typhoon or Rabagliati. Altogether, sixty aircraft were involved in the unsuccessful search. On 31 July 195 Squadron moved to Matlaske and in September 1943 they left Coltishall for Fairlop.

Meanwhile, Spitfire IXs of 611 Squadron sojourned at Ludham for a few days in July and August. Their stay was cut short as Ludham was scheduled for upgrading to await the arrival of a USAAF fighter group. Three concrete runways and fifty new dispersals of 'PSP USAAF type' were constructed, but although the airfield was officially allocated to VIIIth Fighter Command the Americans never took up the option on the airfield. Neither did the Fleet Air Arm, though in August 1944 Ludham was renamed HMS *Flycatcher* with the intention of installing a mobile naval airfield organization. On 16 February 1945 Ludham returned to RAF control in exchange for Middle Wallop. Shortly thereafter 602 and 603 Squadrons arrived with Spitfire XVIs to fly offensive sorties and engage enemy shipping jointly with Coastal Command Beaufighters. These Spitfire squadrons departed in April 1945 to be replaced by 91 Squadron's Spitfire XXIs from Manston, which were joined by 1 Squadron's Spitfires in May. In July the Spitfires left and in September Ludham was briefly allotted to 60 Group before the airfield was decommissioned.

In 1954 location scenes for the film *Conflict of Wings* were shot over a period of about four weeks in and around Hickling Broad, with Ludham village, Catfield's Staithe boat dyke, Cley and Wells being featured. In the film a DH Vampire squadron newly stationed in Norfolk before flying to Malaya to fight jungle terrorists needs a firing range to hone rocket-firing skills but when the RAF tries to requisition a local bird sanctuary for the task it meets stiff opposition from the locals. The film starred John Gregson and Muriel Pavlow (who also played Douglas Bader's wife in *Reach For the Sky* starring Kenneth More and starred in *The Malta Story* and other films). Kieron Moore played the squadron commander. During filming on the broadland waterways actor Harry Fowler managed to steer a motorboat straight into the camera boat, sinking it and hurtling the occupants into the water. The RAF station at Horsham St Faith was also used for film footage of the Vampire and Swift (Supermarine, not the feathered variety) aircraft movements.

MARHAM

Marham aerodrome was first opened in 1916 as a military night-landing ground, covering 80 acres, within the boundary of the present-day aerodrome. From September 1916 units of 31 Squadron were stationed here, flying on home-defence patrols with an assortment of biplane fighters to intercept Zeppelin airships over eastern England. After the First World War Marham was closed and aerodrome construction did not begin until the first half of 1933 when the RAF expansion programme began. By July 1936 work was progressing well: two new public roads had been laid down round the aerodrome to replace country lanes that used to run across the site, including Old Dibbles Drove. When completed the aerodrome was a completely self-contained

A Wellington III of 115 Squadron which crashed near the airfield in 1942. (*Jack Goad via Don Bruce*)

township, with 13 acres of playing fields, a combined church and cinema, fire station, sick quarters, shops, stores and even prison cells with an exercise yard, beside the clutch of hangars. Materials used included 6½ million bricks, 3,000 tons of cement, 40,000 tons of ballast and sand, a million tiles and slates, 100,000 square feet of glass, 2,000 tons of lead, 30 miles of electricity cable, 7 miles of salt-glazed drain pipes and 20 tons of nails. The aerodrome opened as planned on 1 April 1937 as a heavy bomber station in 5 Group, Bomber Command.

No.38 Squadron arrived on 5 May 1937 equipped with twin-engined Fairey Hendon biplane bombers. A month later 115 Squadron re-formed at Marham and began to receive Handley Page Harrows. While these were being delivered, the squadron borrowed some Hendons from 38 Squadron to become operational. After two months, all the Harrows had arrived and both squadrons spent the next two years working up and taking part in the pre-war exercises. In December 1938 38 Squadron re-equipped with Wellington I bombers, followed in April 1939 by 115 Squadron. On 1 June 1939 1 RNZAF Unit had begun forming at Marham to fly Wellingtons. A decision had been taken early in 1937 that the New Zealanders would have a complement of thirty Wellingtons, six of which would be ready to leave for the antipodes in August 1939. When war clouds gathered the New Zealanders were put at the disposal of the RAF and the unit moved to RAF Harwell where it became 15 OTU.

One of the first 5 Group operations of the Second World War

was by seven Wellingtons of 115 Squadron, three from 38 Squadron and others of 149 Squadron from Mildenhall, when they made a daylight attack on German warships near Heligoland on 3 December 1939. Both squadrons took part in coastal patrols and leaflet raids. In April 1940 115 Squadron supported Coastal Command in the Norwegian campaign with an attack on the cruisers *Köln* and *Konigsberg* off Bremen but without success. On 11 November 1940 a force of thirty-six Wellingtons – some from Marham – bombed Waalhaven airfield near Rotterdam, which had earlier been captured by German paratroops. That same night other aircraft from Marham raided Hamburg and on 15 May Wellingtons made an attack on the Ruhr. It was not all one-sided however; during June and July Marham was on the receiving end of two evening raids by the *Luftwaffe*, although no damage was done. During this period Marham's satellite airfield at Barton Bendish and the decoy airfield at South Pickenham were active.

In November 1940 38 Squadron flew to Malta and within two days had been replaced by an advance party of 218 Squadron, which became operational with Wellingtons in December 1940. On 4 and 30 March and 13/14 and 25 April 1941 both squadrons raided Brest, their target being the German battle-cruisers *Scharnhorst* and *Gneisenau*. In January 1941 enemy aircraft, attacked Marham but caused no casualties, but during the next raid on 9 July 1941 two airmen were injured. During August 1941 115 Squadron started the first service trials of Gee, one of the new secret radar aids. A new unit, 1418 Flight, was formed at Marham with four Wellingtons in December 1941 to develop it

Wellington III Z1657/R (formerly A-Apple, as retained on the nose) near Lady Wood, Marham in August–September 1942. (*Jack Goad via Don Bruce*)

Mosquito B.IVs of 105 Squadron at Marham on 11 December 1942. The squadron operated from the airfield from 22 September 1942 until 23 March 1944. (*IWM*)

before it went into widespread use. This flight moved to Tempsford on 1 March 1942. During January and February 1942 meanwhile, the Wellingtons of 218 Squadron were replaced by Short Stirlings, the first of the four-engined heavies used by the RAF in the Second World War. On 12 May Marham was attacked five times by German raiders; buildings damaged included the sergeants' mess. Marham aircraft also took part in Gardening operations in early 1942, the mining of enemy sea-lanes.

On 30 May 1942 aircraft from Marham took part in the first 1,000-bomber raid. Seventeen Wellingtons of 115 Squadron followed by 22 Stirlings of 218 Squadron took off from Marham that night. Some senior officers from 3 Group HQ at Mildenhall accompanied the Marham crews, including Air Vice Marshal John Baldwin, the AOC of 3 Group. Nine Hundred bombers reached Cologne, where over 2,400 tons of bombs were dropped which devastated 600 acres of the city. Thirty-nine bombers failed to return. No.218 Squadron left for Downham Market on 7 July 1942. No.1483 (Bomber) Gunnery Training Flight arrived a week later with Wellington Ic and III and Defiant I and II aircraft to

Flying Officer A. B. 'Smokey Joe' Stovel RCAF of 139 Squadron gets a light from his navigator, Sergeant W. A. Nutter before setting off in Mosquito B.IV DZ593/K on 27 May 1943 to bomb the Schott glass works at Jena with five other Mosquitoes. A few miles further on eight Mosquitoes of 105 Squadron bombed the Zeiss optical factory. Stovel made it back and landed at 2340 hours. (*via Peter Pereira*)

train bomb aimers and air gunners who came directly from training schools without going to OTUs. The bomb aimers in particular performed exercises using Gee before the flight returned to Newmarket Heath on 29 June 1943. No.1427 Training Flight moved to Marham with Stirlings on 4 August 1942. This flight, which moved to Stradishall on 2 October 1942, trained Air Transport Auxiliary (ATA) pilots on four-engined bombers. No.115 Squadron left for Mildenhall on 24 September 1942.

Marham was transferred to 2 Group, Bomber Command, in September 1942, and 105 and 139 Squadrons arrived with the Mosquito Conversion Unit (CU) from Horsham St Faith. No.105 was equipped with Mosquito Mk IV bombers and 139 were then converting to this type from Blenheim V (Bisleys), while the Mosquito CU flew a mixture of Blenheims and Mosquitoes. (On 18 October the CU was renamed the Mosquito Training Unit.) On 19 September 105 Squadron attempted the first daylight Mosquito raid on Berlin. Only one crew succeeded in bombing the 'Big City', two others having to release their bombs on Hamburg after finding Berlin covered by cloud, and the fourth was shot down. Six days later, on 25 September, four Mosquitoes of 105 Squadron led by Squadron Leader George Parry and flying from Leuchars in Scotland, bombed the *Gestapo* HQ in Oslo, Norway, for the loss of one of the Mosquitoes. At least four bombs entered the roof of the building. One had remained inside and failed to detonate and the three others crashed through the opposite wall before exploding. By the end of November 1942 105 Squadron had flown 282 operational sorties and lost 24 aircraft.

On 6 December 1942 2 Group mounted its biggest operation of the war when ninety-three light bombers attacked the Philips Strijp Group main works and the Emmasingel valve and lamp factory in Eindhoven, Holland, from low-level. Ten Mosquitoes, led by Wing Commander Hughie Edwards VC DFC, trailed the Bostons and Venturas to the target, where the Mosquitoes made a shallow diving attack. One Mosquito, nine Venturas and four Bostons were lost. On 27 January 1943 Hughie Edwards led nine Mosquitoes of 105 Squadron in daring low-level strikes on the Burmeister and Wain Diesel engine works at Copenhagen. Edwards found the target only at the last moment and was on the point of returning but they hit it and then broke for the sea and home. On 31 January Mosquitoes got their bombs away over Berlin for the first time. Two attacks – one in the morning and one in the afternoon – were timed to disrupt speeches in the main broadcasting station in Berlin by *Reichsmarschall* Herman

Crews of 139 Squadron beside Mosquito IV DZ470 N-Nuts on compass swing at Marham in the spring of 1943. (*via Peter Pereira*)

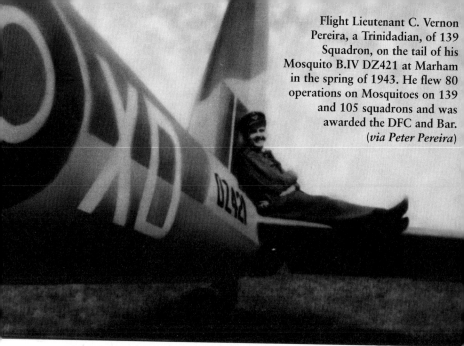

Flight Lieutenant C. Vernon Pereira, a Trinidadian, of 139 Squadron, on the tail of his Mosquito B.IV DZ421 at Marham in the spring of 1943. He flew 80 operations on Mosquitoes on 139 and 105 squadrons and was awarded the DFC and Bar. (*via Peter Pereira*)

Göring and Dr Joseph Göbbels. Three Mosquitoes of 105 attacked in the morning and in the afternoon three Mosquitoes of 139 Squadron set out. No.105 Squadron arrived over the 'Big City' at exactly 1100 hours and their bombs rained down, disrupting Göring's speech for over an hour, but the afternoon raid was not as successful and one Mosquito was shot down. The final large-scale daylight raid by 105 and 139 Squadrons was on 27 May 1943 when the Zeiss optical factory and the Schott glass works at Jena were attacked. (On 30 April 1943 1655 Mosquito TU disbanded at Marham and relocated to Warboys.)

On 1 June 1943 Marham came under the control of 8 Group and 105 and 139 Squadrons were the first Mosquito units to join the specialist Pathfinder Force (later 8 (PFF) Group). On 4 July 139 Squadron left for Wyton, being replaced the same day by 109 Squadron, which flew Mosquito IVs and IXs. Within 8 Group 105 and 109 Squadrons flew on night operations and as pathfinders for the main force of bombers, using the *Oboe* blind bombing device. The first use of *Oboe* by 105 Squadron was on the night of 9/10 July 1943 when two aircraft bombed Gelsenkirchen. On the night of 25/26 July 1943, nine Mosquitoes of 109 squadron dropped markers on the Krupps armament works at Essen for the main force of 600 bombers, which caused severe damage to the target. Other targets included the ball-bearing works at Elberford, storage dumps and fighter airfields. On 23 March 1944 105 Squadron left for Bourn while in April 109 Squadron left for Little Staughton. With the departure of these squadrons, Marham closed to allow concrete runways, perimeter track and dispersals to be laid and this marked the end of its use as a wartime airfield. In January 1946 the runway was completed and flying began again.

MATLASKE

In October 1940 the increasing vulnerability of parked fighters at Coltishall led to Matlaske, 12 miles north-west of the host station near Holt and about 6 miles south-west of Cromer, becoming the first of the host station's two satellite airfields in the county (the other being Ludham). In reality Coltishall and Matlaske would operate as one. Operations from within the clutch stations of Coltishall, Matlaske and Ludham were integrated. Squadrons from Duxford were often moved forward on a daily basis to replace any of Coltishall's resident squadrons, which were sent to other sectors. Matlaske had two runways built – one 1,600 yards long and the other 1,300. The airfield was built in such great haste that there were severe drainage problems throughout the airfield's wartime life and living quarters had not been completed by the time that 72 Squadron with Spitfire Is arrived late in October. Living quarters and air-raid shelters for the airmen ware built in the grounds of Barningham Park, while the officers were

On 2 July 1941 601 Squadron arrived at Matlaske from Manston with Hurricane IIb fighters, flying several bomber escort operations and fighter sweeps over Europe until August when it began to re-equip with the Bell Airacobra I. After a few days the squadron moved to Duxford. (*IWM*)

Westland Whirlwind I P7048 of 137 Squadron, the second squadron to be equipped with the type after 263 Squadron had become operational in December 1940. (*Charles E. Brown*)

billeted in requisitioned Barningham Hall, which after the staircase and fireplaces were boxed in, became home for both air and ground crews. Described as 'charming', it was a far cry from the accommodation available at permanent stations throughout Norfolk. Ironically, on 29 October five *Luftwaffe* aircraft bombed and strafed Matlaske airfield.

No.72 Squadron's Spitfire Is left in early November and 222 Squadron, who detached their Spitfires here from Coltishall, replaced them. These were sometimes used for Kipper patrols to protect the local fishing fleet. On 6 May 1941 the whole of 222 Squadron was stationed at Matlaske and they remained until 30 June. On 2 July 1941 601 Squadron arrived from Manston with Hurricane IIb fighters, flying several bomber escort operations and fighter sweeps over Europe until August when the squadron started to re-equip with the new American fighter, the Bell Airacobra I. After a few days this squadron moved to Duxford. The same month 19 Squadron arrived with Spitfires, moving to Ludham in December 1941. The close proximity of Coltishall to the sea made an ideal location for ASR operations. In July 1941 5 ASR Flight was formed with two Supermarine Walrus

Westland Whirlwind Is of 137 Squadron at Matlaske. On 8 November 1941 137 Squadron arrived at Coltishall from Charmy Down, Somerset, having been formed in September with Westland Whirlwind I fighters. It began operations with coastal patrols and convoy escorts almost immediately off Yarmouth and the east coast. On 1 December the Whirlwinds moved to Matlaske to continue operations until 24 August 1942. (*Mick Jennings Coll*)

amphibians and became 278 Squadron at Matlaske in October when Westland Lysander IIIs, Boulton Paul Defiant Is and Avro Anson Is were added. Detachments were sent to Coastal Command stations as far afield as Acklington in Northumberland and Sumburgh in the Shetlands. From 10 April 1942 278 Squadron operated from Coltishall with detachments at Matlaske, until on 21 April 1944 the unit moved to Bradwell Bay in Essex.

During the winter of 1941/42 seventeen blister hangars were erected at Matlaske. On 1 December 1941 137 Squadron's Westland Whirlwind Is arrived from Coltishall to fly fighter sweeps and coastal patrols. On 12 February 1942 the Whirlwinds were sent to escort destroyers, finding instead the *Scharnhorst* and *Gneisenau,* and the Bf 109 escort shot down three aircraft. The Whirlwind squadron's first victory came on 25 June and in August the squadron moved to Manston. The same month 56 Squadron arrived with Typhoon Ia and Ib fighters, using these for 'Circuses' and 'Rhubarbs' (bomber escorts and fighter sweeps respectively). This squadron sometimes operated from Coltishall

Westland Whirlwind Is of 137 Squadron at Matlaske. Whirlwinds were not successful and were withdrawn from operations in 1943. (*Mick Jennings Coll*)

and Ludham. One of the first accidents involving a Typhoon came on 24 August 1942 when P7585 overshot the grass runway, crashed into a tractor and was written off. One of the first Typhoon combats was on 14 September 1942 when a pair of 56 Squadron aircraft, flown by Flight Lieutenant M. lngle-Finch and Pilot Officer W. H. Coombes found a Ju 88 flying beneath low cloud off the Norfolk coast. Coombes attacked first followed by two attacks by Ingle-Finch who nearly collided with the Junkers. Coombes made two more attacks to finish it off and it was last seen diving into cloud trailing smoke and debris and was claimed 'destroyed'.

Three Typhoons of 56 Squadron carried out a 'Rhubarb' on 17 November 1942, attacking flak posts, an airfield, a train and billets. One Canadian pilot, Bob Deugo, reported hitting a German gunner on the head with his wing as he scrambled up over some sandbags to escape. On return a dent was found in the leading edge of his Typhoon's wing. On 1 October 1942 two Typhoons of 56 Squadron at Matlaske approached Coltishall and circled the airfield. One of the Typhoons, R7711/M flown by Pilot Officer Wright, had burst a tyre on take-off from Matlaske. Squadron Leader 'Cocky' Dundas, 56 Squadron commander, was airborne at the time and decided that the young inexperienced pilot should not attempt an emergency landing on the undulating runways at Matlaske. So, with his squadron commander at his side, Wright flew the few miles to Coltishall to attempt his landing. His approach was fine but as soon as the wheels touched the grass-covered matting his Typhoon bounced and turned turtle. His aircraft was a write-off but luckily Wright escaped with a broken limb. He was involved in two further potentially fatal accidents, both times escaping by parachute. In fact he later boasted that he had broken more Typhoons than anyone else had!

The King and Queen visited Matlaske on 28 January 1943 and inspected 56 Squadron. During that month Squadron Leader Pheloung, a New Zealander, became CO. Shortly afterwards he was shot down by a flak ship and baled out into the North Sea. He was later picked up and returned to Matlaske. On 20 June 1943 he was again shot down off the Dutch coast by anti-aircraft fire, but this time he did not return.

On 2 September 1942 Matlaske was allocated to the 8th Air Force as a fighter base (Station 178) and during March and April 1943 the 56th Fighter Group were based there with P-47D

Hawker Typhoon Ib EK183 of 56 Squadron which was stationed at Matlaske from 24 August 1942 to 22 July 1943 for 'Circuses' and 'Rhubarbs'. This squadron sometimes operated from Coltishall and Ludham and returned to Matlaske in September1944 with Tempest Vs. (*via Paul Wilson*)

Thunderbolts under the command of Colonel Hubert Zemke. The 56th Fighter Group moved to Horsham St Faith during July 1943. From March to May 1943 a detachment of 245 Squadron was stationed here with Typhoon Ibs. During July 1943 611, 195 and 609 Squadrons arrived. No.611 Squadron was here for a few weeks while working up on Spitfire LFVbs; 195 and 609 were equipped with Typhoons. No.195 had previously been stationed at Ludham, where they had operated against the Fw 190 hit-and-run raiders. On 29 July 1943 as 118 Squadron aircraft returned to Coltishall from Matlaske, two of their Spitfires collided in a formation break as they prepared to land, and both pilots were killed. Nos 195 and 609 Squadrons left Matlaske in August 1943.

Matlaske was a grass-covered airfield, but later in the war Summerfeld net tracking made in Norwich by Boulton Paul formed the runways. The station had a relatively quiet time from August 1943 until September 1944 when 3, 56 and 486 Squadrons arrived with Tempest Vs, which may have been used on anti-V-1 patrols – all three squadrons leaving the same month. They were replaced by three Mustang squadrons – 19, 65 and 122, flying day-bomber escort duties. Early in October the Mustang squadrons were replaced by 229, 453 RAAF and 602 Squadrons equipped with Spitfire IXs, using these for day-bomber escort and fighter sweeps. No.229 Squadron left in

November 1944 while the two other squadrons received Spitfire XVIs. In February 1945 602 Squadron left temporarily, returning the same month and both squadrons finally left in April 1945. The station closed in October 1945.

OULTON

The site of Oulton airfield was requisitioned early in 1940 and when completed it opened in July as a satellite landing ground for Horsham St Faith controlled by 2 Group, Bomber Command. When on 9 August 1940 German bombers raided St Faith, hitting hangars and aircraft, the next day 114 Squadron and its Blenheim IVs were moved to the north-east Norfolk airfield. (Further attacks were made again on St Faith that evening.) No.114 Squadron's main targets were the Channel ports and targets in occupied Europe and Germany. On 15 December 2 Group's Blenheims took part in a major attack on Mannheim. Blenheim IV R3744 of 114 Squadron had engine failure on take-off from Oulton and jettisoned two 250-lb HE bombs on Norwich before crashing at Sprowston. No.114 flew bombing operations from Oulton until March 1941 when it was sent to Thornaby for operations in support of Coastal Command. No.2 Group then moved 18 Squadron's Blenheims to Oulton from Great Massingham on 3 April. The majority of the aircrews were initially housed in local dwellings, but a fortunate few were billeted in Blickling Hall nearby. One of them was Blenheim gunner Sergeant Jim 'Dinty' Moore, who recalls:

Our accommodation could not have been less like that which we had enjoyed at Massingham, for we now found ourselves living in the beautiful Blickling Hall, the home of landed gentry since the time of the Doomsday Book. The sergeants' mess was situated in what is now the Steward's Room, the entrance being in the south-west corner of the Hall. The main entrance and the staircase were not accessible to us but the remainder of the hall and all the grounds were our 'home'. The officers' mess was located in the east wing of the Hall with the entrance in the south-east corner. We occupied about two-thirds of the house and most of the buildings in the grounds, with access to the acres of grounds and the lake in which we were able to swim, despite the presence of a large swan who appeared to resent

89

our presence. The estate even had its own church and a small public house. The wing commander had a very grand room, which, it was said, had been occupied by Anne Boleyn, overlooking the park and the lake. Many of the estate employees still lived in their cottages and must have found our presence somewhat different from anything to which they had become accustomed. On one memorable occasion one of our colleagues, having spent the evening in Norwich imbibing more than his share of the local ale, took a fancy to one of those large yellow balls on the top of a pedestrian crossing sign. He purloined this, bringing it back joyfully to the hall, where he deposited it in the garden. The following morning the head gardener emerged from his cottage and, having heard warnings of explosive devices being dropped by the Luftwaffe *hurriedly alerted the bomb squad. On their arrival these gentlemen were not impressed and their comments are unprintable!*

No.18 Squadron moved to Horsham St Faith in July and 139 Squadron's Blenheims arrived for a stay of three months No.18 Squadron returned to Oulton again in November for a few weeks before they returned once more to Horsham. On 5 December 1941 139 Squadron returned to Oulton to convert to Lockheed Hudson GR.IIIs administered by 1428 Flight, which had been formed in late December 1941. On 18 December Hudson III V9231 crashed on take-off from Oulton. On January 28 1942 Hudson III V9098 crashed when it failed to take off due to icing. No.1428 Flight disbanded on 29 May 1942. Some of the 139 Squadron Blenheim IV crews, meanwhile, had been posted to Malta in December 1941, where the squadron lost its identity. In June 1942, however, 139 re-formed in 2 Group with Mosquito IV day bombers.

During the summer of 1942 Oulton was loaned to Coastal Command and 236 Squadron arrived with Beaufighter Ic aircraft in July. The Beaus had only recently been fitted with underwing carriers for two 250 pound bombs and it was in the process of conducting trials using the aircraft in the torpedo-bomber role against enemy shipping off the Dutch coast. The trials were so successful that in September 236 Squadron was transferred to North Coates to form part of the first Beaufighter Strike wing.

That same month work began on bringing Oulton up to Class A standard and the airfield became the satellite to Swanton

Morley in 2 Group. Douglas Boston IIIs of 88 Squadron arrived from Attlebridge on 30 September. Among the crews was Pilot Officer Jim Moore.

After having flown many hours in Blenheims we found the Douglas Boston a really first-class twin-engined medium bomber, ideally suited for low-level flying, highly manoeuvrable, faster and carrying a larger bomb load than the dear old Blenheim. It also meant living in Blickling Hall again, which for me was like going home, except that this time I lived in the officers' mess with the services of a batman!

On 6 December Wing Commander Pelly-Fry, 88 Squadron CO, led Operation *Oyster*, the 2 Group low-level daylight raid on the Philips radio and valve works in Eindhoven. In all, ninety-one aircraft (thirty-six Bostons, fourty-seven Venturas and eight Mosquitoes) took part. No.88 Squadron contributed twelve Bostons, which together with twelve of 226 Squadron and seventeen Venturas of 21 Squadron bombed the Emmasingel valve factory.)

In the spring of 1943 we spent some time converting from the Boston III to the IIIa. It was a period of preparation for the invasion of Europe and the development of close links with the army, to which the group would provide close support. On 1 April 1943 our days of living in the splendour of Blickling Hall came to an end and we moved the few miles to Swanton Morley. On the plus side, the food in the officers' mess was excellent, as the chef had formerly been employed in a leading London hotel.

No.21 'City of Norwich' Squadron, which arrived at Oulton in April from Methwold when that station was returned to 3 Group, was equipped with Ventura B.I/III bombers. These were used mainly for attacking targets in occupied Europe until the Squadron left for Sculthorpe in September to convert to the Mosquito FBVI. No.2 Group now became part of Second Tactical Air Force and all 2 Group's airfields in Norfolk were then transferred to 3 Group control, though on 16 March 1944 Oulton opened in 100 Group, Bomber Command. (*See also Blickling Hall.*)

SCULTHORPE

One of the three aerodromes making up the 'West Raynham Clutch, construction at Sculthorpe was begun by Bovis and Constable Hart & Co at the end of 1942 to Class A standard. In January 1943 the first operational unit to arrive was 342 'Lorraine' Squadron, recently formed at West Raynham with French personnel flying Boston IIIAs. The squadron spent its first weeks at Sculthorpe continuing training and flying their Bostons from West Raynham until 15 May when the runway triangle at Sculthorpe was completed. The same day B-17F 42-29852 *Fireball* of the 351st Bombardment Group at Polebrook became the first American aircraft to use Sculthorpe when it made an emergency landing returning from the mission to Emden. A crewman who had baled out was trailing helplessly behind the B-17 with his canopy caught on the tail unit. He was pulled back inside but was found to be dead on landing.

On 19 July the Free French moved to Great Massingham to make room for three Ventura squadrons, 487 RNZAF and 464 RAAF at Methwold and 21 Squadron at Oulton, who began conversion to the Mosquito FBVI. By the end of September conversion was complete and 487 and 464 Squadrons became operational in October and 21 Squadron a month later. On 31

The airfield pictured in June 1994. (*Author*)

December 1943 all three squadrons of 140 Wing took off from Sculthorpe for the last time, bombed Le Ploy, France and returned to land at their new station at Hunsdon.

On 16 January 1944 214 Squadron re-formed at Sculthorpe to convert to the Boeing Fortress and an RCM role in 100 Group. Initial equipment included a few war-weary USAAF Fortresses, two ex-Coastal Command Fortress Is and Fortress II (B-17F) aircraft that were delivered from Scottish Aviation Ltd at Prestwick, where they had been used on night operations and were painted black overall. Removal of the ball turret, flame dampers, and fitting of British communication and oxygen equipment took place and the bomb bay was fitted out with Airborne Cigar (ABC) and later, Jostle, jamming equipment. No.214 Squadron were joined by 803rd Bombardment Squadron USAAF, which helped the RAF crews convert to the Fortress, and later the RAF crews helped the Americans convert to the British equipment. The Stars and Stripes and RAF ensign were lowered fro the last time on 2 October 1992 to bring to an end one of Europe's largest nuclear bomber bases and the home for countless military exercises.

SWANTON MORLEY

This airfield, overlooking the south side of the Wensum valley is unique to the region in that until its closure on 6 September 1995, it had the largest RAF grass airfield in Europe. On 15 September, Battle of Britain Day 1995, appropriately, Swanton Morley's station ensign was lowered for the last time and fifty-five years of history came to an end.

In the late 1930s Swanton Morley was an expansion scheme airfield but it was never finished to the usual standard. With war imminent work on improving it's overall facilities, which would cost a total of £490,000, began. Buildings were erected by Richard Costain & Co Ltd near Mill Street on the eastern side of the airfield. Several country roads, especially between the villages of Worthing and Swanton Morley, were closed. Between 1941 and 1943 four T2 hangars were erected on the airfield and thirty-one loop hardstandings and a perimeter track were laid. (When work on barracks was finished 1,968 airmen and 390 WAAFs could be accommodated.) But on 17 September 1940, when the airfield opened in 2 Group Bomber Command, it was only partly finished, with the only hangarage being a single Type J hangar that had been erected on the technical site. During the next few months tarmac hardstandings were laid around the perimeter of the grass airfield.

The first unit to move to Swanton Morley was 105 Squadron, which had lost most of its Fairey Battle aircraft in the Battle of France and was in the process of receiving Blenheim IV light bombers. The Blenheim squadrons suffered heavy losses during 1940 and 1941, and 105 Squadron was no exception. Between 3 and 30 June 1941 22 Blenheims of 2 Group were lost with 56 aircrew killed and 6 taken prisoner, mainly on anti-shipping strikes off the enemy coast. On 27 June ten crews from 107 Squadron flew to Swanton Morley for a special briefing where they and ten crews of 105 were told that they would carry out a low-level attack on the docks at Bremen the following day. This involved flying over the German mainland for 105 miles, far beyond the range of fighter protection. The formation lost the essential element of surprise and turned back. Crews tried again on 4 July when Operation *Wreckage*, led by Australian Wing Commander Hughie Edwards DFC, CO of 105 Squadron went ahead. At the target flak and balloons split the formation and about twenty shells found their mark on Edwards's Blenheim. Two 105 Squadron machines and two of 107 Squadron were shot down and every other aircraft was damaged. The raid however was deemed successful. Edwards then circled Bremen and strafed a stationary train that had opened up on them, before leading the formation out of Germany at low level. Edwards, his aircraft minus part of the port wing, the port aileron badly damaged, a cannon shell in the radio rack and a length of telegraph wire wrapped round the tail wheel and trailing behind, headed for Bremerhaven and Wilhelmshaven. More flak rose to greet them at Bremerhaven until finally the coastline at Heligoland came into view and the Blenheims dived down to sea level again. The battered formation flew north of the Friesians for a short time then headed westwards for Swanton Morley, where Edwards put down safely. On 21 July it was announced that Hughie Edwards had been awarded the VC for courage and leadership displayed on the Bremen operation.

At the end of August 152 Squadron with Spitfire IIs arrived to share escort duties on 2 Group raids until the end of the year. During July and August 88 Squadron operated Blenheims at

RAF Swanton Morley, with the main camp top left of the grass airfield, now Robertson Barracks. Bottom centre is the RAF 100 Group Mosquito servicing hangar. (*RAF*)

Swanton before moving to Attlebridge to convert to the Boston III. No.105 Squadron was also due for re-equipment but not to the Boston. On 15 November Geoffrey de Havilland Jr in a Mosquito treated them to a breathtaking display. W4066, the first Mosquito bomber to enter RAF service, arrived at Swanton Morley on 17 November but re-equipment by Mosquito BIVs was a drawn out affair and Swanton Morley's grass airfield and unfinished state proved unsuitable. On 9 December, therefore, 105 Squadron moved to Horsham St Faith near Norwich.

To take their place, 226 Squadron, commanded by Wing Commander V. S. Butler DFC arrived from Wattisham, where they had been flying Blenheims, and they were soon thrown into

On 19 July 1942 twenty Bostons of 88 and 226 Squadrons mounted raids in pairs on ten power stations in the Lille area using low cloud as cover. Z2236, flown by Pilot Officer Aubrey K. C. Niner of 88 Squadron, was one of two aircraft given a power station at Lille-Lomme but the crew were unable to locate the target and so they bombed the airfield at Lille-Nord instead. Hits were scored on a hangar before Z2236 was hit in the starboard engine by flak and Niner had to belly-land on a football pitch in Lille. Niner, the Wop/AG, Sergeant George Lawman, and the navigator, Flight Sergeant Philip Jacobs were taken prisoner. (*Aubrey Niner*)

action although conversion to Boston IIIs was far from complete. Operation *Fuller* was mounted on 12 February in a vain attempt to prevent the 'Channel Dash' by the *Scharnhorst, Gneisenau* and *Prinz Eugen*, which were slipping through the English Channel from their French berths to Germany. Six of 226 Squadron's Bostons and four from 88 were involved (as were thirty-seven Blenheims). Only one crew found the German ships and escorting fighters beat them off. The pilot landed at Swanton Morley with two holes in the fuselage and an unexploded 20 mm cannon shell in the starboard wing. The first Boston operation took place on 8 March when six Bostons of 226 Squadron led by Wing Commander Butler and six of 88 Squadron at Attlebridge made the first daylight bombing raid of the war on Paris. The target, the Ford motor works at Matford near Poissy on the banks of the Seine was turning out tanks and military vehicles for the Germans. Butler was shot down and killed. Damage to the Matford works put it out of commission for three months.

In June 226 Squadron hosted the A-20 crews of the 15th Light

Mitchell IIIs FV905/S – *Stalingrad*, FW130/A and FW128/H of 226 Squadron, which became operational at Swanton Morley at the end of July 1943. (*via A. S. Thomas*)

Bombardment Squadron USAAF, who, being the only American unit in the UK at the time and with Independence Day looming, were needed for a flag-waving curtain-raiser to an American offensive in Europe. The first 8th Air Force involvement in a mission to drop bombs on an enemy target was on 4 July 1942, when six of the twelve A-20 Bostons belonging to 226 Squadron carried American crews in attacks on four airfields in Holland.

Throughout September and October 1942 pairs of Bostons from 88, 107 and 226 Squadrons continued low-level attacks on power stations in northern France. Twenty-year-old Sergeant

In the haunted former services' cinema at Swanton Morley are cartoons of men fencing...

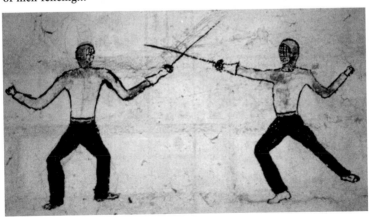

...a 'Desperate Dan' character...

...a duck...

...A young lady. (*Author*)

(later Warrant Officer) Maurice 'Collie' Collins was a Boston pilot in 226 Squadron, much of whose time since joining the squadron at Swanton Morley was spent on formation flying, low-level flying and gunnery practice. He recalls: 'No.2 Group sent aircraft to look for pocket battleships and later to cover the landing at Dieppe but the only raids I went on were ten high-level Circuses and one low level against 'Squealers'. Evenings were spent in Swanton Morley village, the King's Arms in Dereham or the fleshpots of Norwich until the evening of 21 September 1942.' Collins's crew found themselves on a battle order for a low-level raid on power stations early the following morning. The Boston was shot down but Collins evaded capture while his two crew survived to become PoWs. On Sunday, 6 December 1942 twelve Bostons of 226 Squadron took part in Operation Oyster when 2 Group sent ninety-one light bombers to bomb the Philips radio and valve works at Eindhoven. The Bostons released their delayed-action bombs on the Emmasingel valve factory before the Mosquitoes came in behind at 1,000 feet with HE and incendiary bombs. Fourteen aircraft (nine Venturas, one Mosquito and four Bostons) were shot down. Photographs taken after the raid showed that both factories had been very badly damaged, fully justifying the decision to make the attack in daylight from low level.

Unlike most other 2 Group squadrons, 226 was not moved south during summer and autumn 1943 and they were to remain at Swanton Morley until 14 February 1944, when they moved to Hartford Bridge. In April 1943 88 Squadron returned to Swanton Morley, with Boston aircraft this time, and they stayed until 19 August 1943 when they flew to a new aerodrome at Hartford Bridge near Camberley. They were joined there the following day by 107 Squadron from Great Massingham and shortly after by 342 'Lorraine' Squadron to form 137 Wing. Operations from Swanton Morley had resulted in the loss of twenty-one Blenheims and eighteen Bostons.

...a Highland fling...

In 1943 moves were afoot to transfer 2 Group HQ in Bomber Command at Bylaugh Hall nearby and its ten squadrons of light bombers at seven airfields in Norfolk to the 2nd Tactical Air Force (TAF) ready to support the invasion of Europe, which was planned for May and June 1944. (On 18 January 1944 2 Group HQ at Bylaugh Hall nearby moved to Mongewell Park near Wallingford in Berkshire.) No.305 *Ziemia Wielkopolska* Squadron spent September and November 1943 at Swanton having converted from the Wellington to the Mitchell and then on 18 November 1943, the Poles left for Lasham to receive Mosquito FBVIs, joining 107 and 613 'City of Manchester' Squadrons to become part of 138 Wing.

During late November 1943 and February 1944 Typhoons of 3 squadron were stationed at Swanton. On 14 February 1944 226 Squadron, which had converted to Mitchell IIs in mid-1943, flew from Swanton Morley for the last time, when they took off for Hartford Bridge to train for their role in the forthcoming invasion of France. The 2nd TAF would be tasked to destroy tactical rather than strategic targets as and when D-Day arrived, so to be near the invasion front all squadrons were moved further south. In March and April Boston and Mitchell units and Mosquito crews of 464 Squadron RAAF and 487 Squadron RNZAF arrived at 2 GSU (formerly 1482 Bombing and Gunnery Flight) to participate in two-week training exercises in full field conditions. All crews

'Jane' the famous *Daily Mirror* strip cartoon character, still survives in the haunted former cinema at Swanton Morley. (*Author*)

lived under canvas and life was distinctly uncomfortable. To simulate the type of tactical targets 2 Group would be bombing in the run-up to D-Day, night interdictor training (bombing and strafing the enemy's communications), bombing of illuminated targets and convoys and runs on a 'spoof' V1 rocket site and a four-gun flak battery installation were carried out. During a two-week sojourn, on 11 April 1944, six FBVIs of 613 'City of Manchester' Squadron led by Wing Commander R. N. 'Bob' Bateson DFC attacked and completely destroyed the Huize

Mosquito FBVI LR366 of 613 'City of Manchester' Squadron, 138 Wing, 2 Group refuelling at RAF Swanton Morley early in 1944 during night interdictor training at the 2 GSU station. LR366 joined 107 Squadron and failed to return from the Arnhem operation on 17 September 1944 when the Mosquitoes of 138 Wing, 2nd TAF bombed German barracks as part of Operation *Market Garden*. (*via Philip Birtles*)

Kleykamp a five-storey, 95-feet high white building on Carnegie Square in The Hague, which contained *Gestapo* records. An Air Ministry bulletin later described the raid as 'probably the most brilliant feat of low-level precision bombing of the war'. For his leadership of this operation Bateson was awarded the DSO and he received the Dutch Flying Cross from Prince Bernhard of the Netherlands.

Late in October 1944 another daring low-level raid by Mosquitoes, this time on Aarhus University, the *Gestapo* HQ for the whole of Jutland, Denmark, was ordered. The university consisted of four or five buildings just next to an *autobahn*, which ran ten miles in a straight line up to the buildings. Twenty-five FBVIs of 21 Squadron, 464 Squadron RAAF and 487 Squadron RNZAF carried out the precision attack on 31 October; each carrying eleven-second delayed-action bombs. Escort was provided by eight Mustang IIIs of 315 (Polish) Squadron, 12 Group, which flew to Swanton Morley from their base at Andrews Field in Essex, led by the CO, Squadron Leader Tadeusz Andersz. One of the Mustang pilots was Flight Lieutenant Konrad 'Wiewiorka' (Squirrel) Stembrowicz, who recalls:

We landed at Swanton Morley early on the morning of 31 October. One or two of our Mustangs damaged their tailwheels on the grass field and were not ready in time for the escort. Eight of us refuelled and took off again to

Spitfires at Swanton Morley on 1 May 1990 during location shooting for the TV series, *The Perfect Hero*. (*Richard Slipper*)

Thirteen Second World War airmen are buried in All Saints churchyard at Swanton Morley. There are also eight post-war graves, including that of Corporal Hugh Jonathon Spencer (seventeen), Radley College Cadet Force, killed in the crash of Cadet TX3 glider XE804 of 614 Gliding School. The church has a stained-glass window subscribed by RAF Swanton Morley. (*Author*)

rendezvous with the Mosquitoes over the North Sea. When we saw them they were at 100 feet above the waves. Our two Finger Fours formated 50 feet below to starboard and slightly south of them. We crossed Denmark and dropped our auxiliary gallon-90 petrol tanks, which by necessity were only halffilled. Mine fell near a Danish cottage surrounded by a mass of brown, yellow and orange chrysanthemums. People ran out of the house and waved their arms and large white tablecloths as we all roared past. Approaching Aarhus the Mosquitoes lifted slightly. They were to attack down a street west to east. The leading section of four Mustangs went left and we followed ...We saw explosions and very light ack-ack coming up in the Mosquitoes wake. All of us went to the right and put ourselves between the Mosquitoes and the German airfields. This time we were higher. We saw no fighters and the flight home was uneventful.

The attack was carried out at such a low altitude that one

The wartime pill box on the Worthing side of the airfield near the remaining T2 hangar. (*Author*)

Mosquito hit the roof of the building, losing its tailwheel and the port half of the tailplane, but it limped back across the North Sea and managed to land safely. The university and its incriminating records were destroyed.

For the remainder of the war Swanton Morley hosted aircraft and units of 100 Group, which needed facilities to support the comings and goings at its headquarters at Bylaugh Hall close by. Also, the Mosquito Major Servicing Section arrived from West Raynham on 31 December 1943. The Bomber Support Development Unit (BSDU) arrived from Foulsham in June 1944 and was established on the Worthing side of the airfield where a T2 hangar had been erected. (The BSDU developed, tested and produced a whole host of radar and radio equipment for 100 Group). During the period June 1944 to April 1945 BSDU carried out 114 operational sorties in Mosquitoes over the continent to test the various fighter devices.

Little use was made of Swanton Morley until December 1946 when 4 Radio School moved in with Proctor, Prentice and Anson aircraft. The school became in turn 1 Air Signallers and the Air Electronic School and remained at Swanton until late in 1957.

Thereafter, the airfield, still turf-surfaced, was little used for RAF flying, although the camp continued to serve for ground units until its closure on 6 September 1995 and a flying club flourished for several years. In 1996 the army took over the camp and much of the landing ground for Robertson Barracks. The J and T2 hangars were demolished to make way for new AFV buildings.

WATTON

This airfield was constructed with grass runways and had all the standard buildings of the 1930s 'expansion' pattern which included C-type hangars. It became operational in 2 Group with the arrival of 21 and 34 Squadrons in February and March 1939, flying the short-nosed Blenheim I. No.21 Squadron arrived on 2 March 1939, flying their Blenheims in formation from Eastchurch, to begin a period of intensive training which included cross-country flights and bombing practice over the ranges at Berner's Heath, Dengie Flats and Wainfleet. After working up 34 Squadron left for Tengah in the Far East in August 1959. The same month 82 Squadron arrived at Watton, also with Blenheim Is and on 27 August half a dozen Henley target tugs of 'A' Flight, No.1 AACU arrived from Western Zoyland. With war imminent all the aircraft at Watton were 'scattered' for short periods – the Blenheims going to Horsham St Faith and Netheravon and the Henleys to West Raynham and Wattisham, the latter all being

Blenheim I aircraft of 21 Squadron at RAF Watton in June 1939. L1345 went on to serve with 90 and 114 Squadrons and 13 OTU until it went to Finland on 21 July 1940. (*Wartime Watton Museum*)

returned to Western Zoyland on 3 September. At the outbreak of war the 2 Group Squadrons at Watton were designated 79 Wing and were by that time in the process of converting to the long-nosed Blenheim IVs.

During the rapid German advance through France and the Low Countries, Blenheims of 21 and 82 Squadrons from Watton and its satellite airfield at Bodney operated day after day in a vain attempt to try and help stem the advancing armoured columns. On 11 May German armour and motorized infantry were pouring across the River Meuse at Maastricht, where the bridges over the Albert Canal were still intact. After the Fairey Battles and the *Armée de l'Air* had failed to destroy the bridges, twelve Blenheims of 21 Squadron from Watton carried out one further attack that evening. They approached the target at 3,000 feet in the face of a tremendous flak barrage and heavy fighter opposition. Four Blenheims were shot down and the rest were severely damaged. At dawn on 12 May Blenheims of 82 Squadron, which had been standing by at Watton since 0730 hours, took off at 1930 hours for an attack on the Albert Canal near Hasselt. The raid was successful and all the crews returned safely. Nine Blenheims of 21 Squadron flew the last operation of the day, also from Watton. Their target was a road at Tongres, which they bombed at 2040 hours from 7,000 feet. At least two of the Blenheims were damaged by flak but they were able to take

A Blenheim IV of 82 Squadron at RAF Watton in the winter of 1939–40. (*Wartime Watton Museum*)

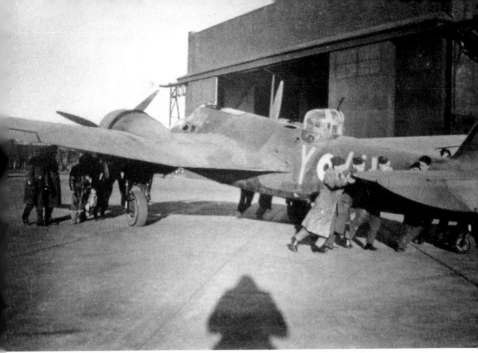

Everyone lends a hand to move Blenheim IV UX-Y of 82 squadron at Watton. (*Wartime Watton Museum*)

advantage of cloud cover for their withdrawal, all of them returning safely.

At 0400 hours on the morning of 17 May twelve crews of 82 Squadron gathered in the briefing room at Watton to be told to attack an enemy column near Gembloux. Their expected fighter escort did not materialize and they ran into a severe flak barrage, which split up the formation, allowing Bf 109s of I/JG3 to attack with great effect. *Oberfeldwebel* Max Bucholz claimed four Blenheims destroyed. Only one Blenheim, flown on one engine and shot to pieces, got back to Watton, the rest being shot down. No.82 Squadron was now non-operational but the CO, Wing Commander the Earl of Bandon (known to all as 'Paddy' and to some as the 'Abandoned Earl') made sure the squadron was re-formed and it resumed operations just three days later. The aircrew displayed tremendous courage in the face of terrible losses, while the ground crews worked ceaselessly, often under impossible conditions, to keep the Blenheims in the air. The rest of May and early June was spent supporting the British Expeditionary Force (BEF). On 21 May nine Blenheims of 21 Squadron and a few of 82 Squadron went in search of enemy

107

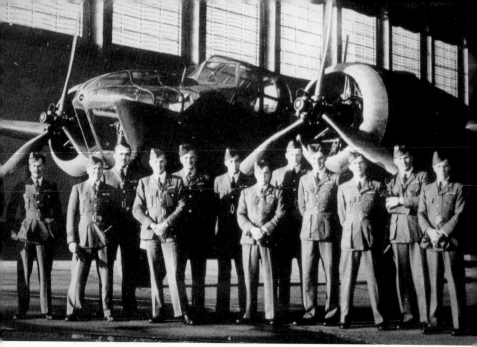

Pilots of 21 Squadron in No.1 Hangar at Watton. Seventh from right is Pilot Officer Ian Stapleton (killed in action in April 1940). (*Wartime Watton Museum*)

transport in the Frevent district, with at least three tanks claimed as hit. Pontoon bridges at Courtrai and Menin in Belgium were the targets for 25 May. The remnants of 18 Squadron arrived at Watton on 19 May 1940 with their remaining Blenheims after being badly mauled in France. After a few days this squadron moved to Gatwick. On 26 May it was decided to evacuate as many troops as possible from Dunkirk, so operations were directed to support the beleaguered BEF forces around the town. Next day the Belgians surrendered. On the last day of May, as the evacuation from Dunkirk reached its climax, the Blenheims in East Anglia flew by far the greatest number of operations on any one day during the campaign. These operations were directed at enemy troops massing for an all-out attack on the evacuation area and it was largely due to their efforts and those of RAF fighter pilots that this attack was halted and the BEF could be evacuated so successfully. In June 21 Squadron was detached to Lossiemouth to fly sorties to Norway, its place being taken by Blenheims of 105 Squadron. No.21 Squadron returned from Lossiemouth in October.

The disaster that befell 82 Squadron in France was repeated on 13 August 1940 when twelve of its crews were briefed to attack Aalborg airfield in Denmark, occupied by Major Fritz Doensch's Ju 88s of I/JG30, which were making sporadic raids on Scotland and northern England. The target was at the extreme limit of the Blenheims' range and pilots were told that they could abort if they ran low on fuel but if they used their 9 pounds of boost to evade fighters, the best they could hope for was to head for Newcastle and put down as near as possible to the coast. At 0845 hours Wing Commander E. C. de Virac Lart DSO led 'A' Flight off from Watton, while 'B' Flight took off from the Bodney satellite field. Over the North Sea the two formations veered slightly off course, taking them many miles south of their intended landfall. At this point Sergeant Baron decided that he would run short of fuel if he continued and he aborted (he was subsequently court martialled but found not guilty).

Blenheim IVs of 82 Squadron at RAF Watton photographed by Sergeant 'Bish' Bareham from the Watton watch office. On 7 June 1940 Sergeant A. E. Merritt and P6915 UX-A (which has one of the first rearward-firing nose guns) returned to Watton so badly shot up by Bf 109s that it was declared beyond repair. Merritt was killed in action six days later. Note the asphalt applied to the grass behind the Blenheims to simulate hedges. (*Wartime Watton Museum*)

Blenheim IV YH-D of 21 Squadron at Watton. This squadron was stationed at Watton from 2 March 1939 to 24 June 1940 (with a detachment at Bodney September 1939–December 1941) and 14 June to 26 December 1941. (*Jack Bartley via Theo Boiten*)

Unfortunately the formation had been identified and its intent correctly deduced. Flak batteries were alerted and eight Bf 109Es of V/JG77 from Stavanger-Sola, which had just flown an escort mission, landed at Aalborg, refuelled and were in the air again as the Blenheims approached. Five Blenheims were shot down by flak and the Bf 109Es of V/JG77 shot down the other five. In all, twenty of the thirty-three Blenheim crewmen (including Lart) were killed and were later buried in the cemetery at Vadum with full military honours. For a second time Wing Commander the Earl of Bandon, a personality whose strength of character held the squadron together at a time when there was precious little of the squadron left to command.

The winter of 1940 saw a temporary switch to night operations in retaliation for the bombing of British cities, and intruder missions were also flown to try and catch some of the *Luftwaffe* bombers returning to their bases. During 1941 their main target was shipping, which if anything was even mere hazardous than the French campaign. Known by the code name *Channel Stop*, the object was to intercept enemy convoys proceeding close inshore to the occupied coasts from the Channel to as far north as Norway. These strikes were mostly carried out at mast height and called for extreme skill on the part of the pilots, who could not afford to make the slightest slip, which could, and often did, end in disaster. Although some success was achieved, the losses in men and machines was very costly for the tonnage of shipping sunk, most casualties being caused by the intense hail of fire thrown up by accompanying flak ships.

Both 21 and 82 Squadrons took their turn in the rota of detachments of 2 Group squadrons to Malta from mid-1941 onwards. Here again the main targets were the Axis convoys plying between Italy and North Africa. Many successful sorties were flown and a high tonnage of shipping sunk, including several oil tankers, which were Rommel's lifeline in the Western Desert. But losses were again grievous and this campaign was halted when the Battle for Malta commenced in early 1942 and the airfields there became virtually untenable for the Blenheim squadrons.

Channel Stop continued well into 1941, while in January of that year the first Circus operations were launched. These were bombing strikes by small formations of Blenheims with very heavy fighter cover, designed to draw enemy fighters to give battle with the intention of holding hack substantial numbers which might otherwise be deployed on other fronts. This type of cooperation was extended over the years and became the bread and-butter line of work for 2 Group. For a short time after February 1941 Oxfords of 15 SFTS used Watton as a relief landing ground and in late April Hampden Is of 'B' Flight, 61 Squadron, were stationed here for a few days. No.90 Squadron was re-formed at Watton on 7 May 1941 to equip with the Boeing Fortress I (B-17C) high-altitude day bomber. After a short working-up period at Watton they moved to West Raynham later that month.

Spitfire IXe MJ175 of 66 Squadron taxiing out at RAF Watton in the winter of 1943/4. MJ175 joined 66 Squadron from 485 Squadron RNZAF at Hornchurch on 8 November 1943 and on 2 April 1944 was written off in a flying accident at Bognor Regis. (*USAF*)

The former RAF Watton today. (*Author*)

In December 1941 21 Squadron left for Malta while on the 20th 1508 Beam Approach Training Flight of 2 Group arrived from Horsham St Faith with Oxfords. This unit stayed for one month, returning to Horsham on 19 January 1942. On 29 January No 17 (Pilots) Advanced Flying Unit ((P) AFU) was formed at Watton with Miles Master trainers. This unit also used Watton's satellite airfield at Bodney. March 1942 saw the final departure of 82 Squadron, which left for India, leaving 17 (P) AFU as the only residents. On 6 November this unit moved to Bodney, with detachments remaining at Watton until 30 June 1943. The station then closed while a concrete runway and new dispersals were laid ready for use by the USAAF, who occupied the station until the war's end. In the summer of 1945 the station reverted to the RAF and Watton was placed under the control of 90 Group. In October 1945 the Radio Warfare Establishment arrived from Swanton Morley equipped with Lancaster, Mosquito and, Proctor aircraft and eight ex-223 Squadron Fortress IIIs, which were finally struck off charge (SOC) in March 1947. In November 1945, 527 Squadron, a radar calibration unit, arrived with Wellington, Oxford and Spitfire aircraft. This squadron disbanded on 15 April 1946. In about June that same year, the Signals Flying Unit (SFU) arrived from Honiley, being stationed at Watton's satellite airfield at Shepherds Grove. The

112

SFU flew Wellingtons, Beaufighters, Oxfords and Ansons to develop, install and calibrate radio aids such as Ground Controlled Approach (GCA). The SFU was absorbed into the Radio Warfare Establishment which in September 1946, was renamed the Central Signals Establishment (CSE).

On 6 September 1950 Watton hosted the annual Battle of Britain air display. Aircraft on display included many piston and jet-engined aircraft while aircraft taking part in the flying display included a Washington B1 of 115 Squadron, three Lincolns of 15 Squadron and the large Short Seaford flying boat which at that time was taking part in trials at the Marine Aircraft Experimental Establishment at Felixstowe.

On 15 July 1951 192 and 199 Squadrons were formed at Watton flying Lincolns and Mosquito NF36 aircraft in the radio countermeasure role as well as on bombing duties. The last Lincolns left in December 1952 and Canberra jet bombers and transport aircraft came and went and the last flying units left in May 1969, Watton becoming the administrative satellite for Honington. Watton aerodrome is now controlled by Commandant of the Stanford Battle Training area and has been renamed STANTA Airfield. It is re-activated almost annually for military co-operation exercises.

Near the side of the now demolished officers' mess is a memorial erected in May 1990 containing two plaques and a twisted propeller recovered from Blenheim R3800, which was shot down at Aalborg, Denmark, on 13 August 1940. Next to it is a memorial dedicated to the memory of the 25th Bomb Group USAAF that also flew from the airfield in the Second World War. (*Author*)

WEST RAYNHAM

This station was a grass airfield during 1938 and 1939, and opened on 5 April 1939 with four Type C hangars and brick buildings north-west of the landing ground. Construction caused the Coxford to Kipton Ash road to be closed to the public. No.2 Group took over the station and on 9 May 1939 101 Squadron arrived, followed the next day by 90 Squadrons both flying a mixture of Blenheim I and IV medium bombers. Upon mobilization the station's squadrons formed 81 Bomber Wing. In early September 1939 both squadrons were scattered: 90 Squadron to Weston-on-the-Green and 101 Squadron to Brize Norton, while Hurricane I fighters of 'B' Flight, 213 Squadron were detached here from Wittering. No.101 Squadron returned after a few days as 2 Group's training squadron. In early October a few Fairey Battle target tugs were acquired by the Station Flight and the following month they were transferred to No.101 Squadron, where aircrew were being posted before joining operational squadrons in the group. During 1940 and 1941, thirty-six pan-type standings were built. No.2 Group continued to use the station and other units also took up residence at various times. In February 1940 the 2 Group Target Tug Flight was formed, allowing 101 Squadron to drop its training role and return to operations by July 1940. During 1940 the flight used

No.101 Squadron was stationed at West Raynham from 6 May 1939 to 1 July 1941 with Blenheim IV aircraft. Pictured is N6165 of 101 Squadron taken by Aircraftman First Class H. Wilson in 1939. (*Wilson Collection via Theo Boiten*)

No.2 Gp TTF operated a number of Fairey Battle II target tugs and other types at West Raynham from October 1939 to March 1941. (*RAF*)

Blenheim I and IVs, Battles, Gladiators and an Avro Tutor, mostly acquired from 101 Squadron.

No.76 Squadron, a 5 Group training unit, was formed at West Raynham on 30 April 1940 with Hampdens and Ansons. This squadron disbanded on 20 May. Five days later the station was bombed for the first time but little damage was done – this was the first of twelve raids. No.139 Squadron arrived on 30 May 1940 for a stay of ten days with Blenheim IVs, its place being taken by 18 Squadron flying a mixture of Blenheim Is and IVs and a few Gladiators as hacks. No.18 Squadron left West Raynham on 9 September.

On 24 November 1940 Blenheim IV N6236 of 101 Squadron, flown by Sergeant B. J. Redmond, crashed on approach near West Raynham village. The aircraft was returning from a raid on the Wanne Eickel oil refinery when it lost a propeller over the North Sea. On 3 January 1941 Blenheim I L1100 of 1 Ferry Pilots Pool hit one of the hangars when taking off and crashed.

The Battles and the Avro Tutor left the 2 Group TT Flight in March 1941. No.90 Squadron returned on 5 May with Boeing Fortress I bombers and was the first and only RAF front-line squadron to fly the type. By the end of May the Fortresses had been detached to the satellite station at Great Massingham and by

115

The airfield and the hangars pictured in June 1994 when the station closed. (*Author*)

June a few Wellington Ic bombers were on the strength of 101 Squadron, carrying out a few raids for 2 Group, including Bremen, Rotterdam, Cologne and Brest.

On 6 June, undoubtedly because of the recent high loss rate, Prime Minister Winston Churchill and other dignitaries visited West Raynham to deliver a morale boosting speech to crews in 2 Group. Flight Sergeant Jim 'Dinty' Moore recalls:

> *Aircraft were lined up for inspection by the great man and two crews of each of the squadrons in the group arrived to take part in this special occasion. In addition to the Bristol Blenheims there were Short Stirling, Handley Page Halifax and Flying Fortress I aircraft and the twin-engined Avro Manchester. 'Winnie' appeared, accompanied by members of the Government and sundry senior officers. He mounted some steps used for the inspection of aircraft engines and invited us to gather round him. We did with alacrity.*

One of his themes was the importance of the work of 2 Group in the war effort and his personal admiration for the courage and persistence of crews undertaking these perilous daylight raids in the face of heavy losses. He went on, 'The Charge of the Light Brigade at Balaclava is eclipsed in brightness by these almost daily deeds of fame.' Ken Wolstenholme of 107 Squadron at Great Massingham recalled, 'I was a sergeant and he was being entertained in the mess. The acoustics were dreadful. When he did speak I was surprised how quiet he was – having heard this strong, resonant voice on the radio. Whether it was because of all the bad news he had been getting or the acoustics I don't know. He came and chatted to the crews – all lined up.'

On 6 July 1941 101 Squadron moved to Oakington, where it joined 3 Group, Bomber Command, and 114 Squadron arrived with Blenheim IVs under the command of Wing Commander J. G. Jenkins DSO DFC. Pilot Officer Charles Patterson was one of the pilots in 114 Squadron at this time.

> *In the middle of July we had to leave Scotland and the comparative safety of the Norwegian coast and rejoin 2 Group in Norfolk for daylight bomber operations. Virtually every operation from now on meant being shot at in some way or other in broad daylight. We flew down to West Raynham in formation. From the moment we landed the whole tempo became more highly charged. We arrived to*

Another picture of the airfield and the hangars pictured in June 1994 when the station closed. (*Author*)

find that our station commander was the famous, ineffable and unique Paddy Bandon, Group Captain the Earl of Bandon, whose personality and achievements were a legend … On Blenheims we lived day to day, each governed by what the bomb load was, your fate designated on the notice board at Weasenham Hall. If you had instantaneous fuses in the bomb load, it meant that you were going on a Circus at medium level. If it was semi-armour-piercing (SAP) eleven-second delay, it meant a low-level shipping attack. Then you simply turned away from the notice board and assumed that your own death warrant had been signed.

Patterson was one of the thirty-eight crews of Force 2 led by Wing Commander James L. 'Nick' Nicol, CO of 114 Squadron, which attacked Knapsack/Oldenburg power station at Cologne on 12 August 1941 when the Quadratfortuna/Cologne power station was also hit. Force 1 lost two Blenheims and Force 2, eight Blenheims. Nicol, who was awarded an immediate DSO for leading the Knapsack raid, was killed on 19 August when his Blenheim was shot down by Bf 110s of II/ZG76 north-west of Vlieland during an attack on a convoy.

During their stay at West Raynham 114 Squadron carried out daylight anti-shipping strikes, daylight sweeps (Circuses), night intruder raids, and night bombing, and occasionally supported British commando raids, including those on Norway. During the night of 26/27 April 1942 Blenheim IV T2430 of 114 Squadron was returning after bombing Eindhoven airfield on a night intruder sortie when it was attacked by a Ju 88 night fighter later identified as a Beaufighter. One engine, the radio and part of the

fuselage was shot out. Further damage caused by anti-aircraft fire in the Lowestoft area made an immediate landing necessary. The Blenheim crash landed at 0155 hours near Thorpe Abbotts village. The crew – Pilot Officer J.R.N. Molesworth RAAF, Pilot Officer L.F.K. Denny and Sergeant Burberry (WOp/AG) – were rounded up by farm workers and taken to a farmhouse where Burberry had his wounds attended to. On 24 July 1942 thirty-six Blenheims including those of 114 Squadrons flew Circus operations to cause a diversion for the bombers attempting to stop the 'Channel Dash' by the *Scharnhorst* and *Gneisenau*. In September 1942 114 Squadron converted briefly to the North American B-25 Mitchell II, only to reconvert to Blenheim V bombers the same month. The Squadron left for Blida in North Africa on 13 November 1942 to take part in Operation 'Torch'.

On 19 July 1941 1420 Flight arrived from Leuchars with Blenheim IVs, disbanding on 15 November 1941. Westland Lysander target tugs joined the 2 Group TT Flight in September 1941. On 14 November 1941 the 2 Group TT Flight was renamed 1482 Target Towing (later Target Towing and Gunnery) Flight. On 1 January 1942 the flight was renamed 1482 (Bomber) Gunnery ((B)G) Flight and in March and April Boston and Defiant aircraft joined the other aircraft of the flight. The Defiants were used for air-to-air gunnery practice.

The North American Mitchell II began to equip 98 Squadron and 180 Squadron, which both re-formed at West Raynham in September 1942 in 2 Group, though the squadrons would not begin flying operations until after they moved to Foulsham on 15 October. Even then, problems with turrets, guns and other systems would delay them further. On 11 November 18 Squadron

The deserted airfield pictured in November 2005. (*Author*)

moved to Algeria. The same month Blenheim IV, Ventura and Martinet aircraft joined 1482 (B) G Flight, the latter type replacing the Lysanders.

On 1 April 1943 342 'Lorraine' Squadron, which was commanded by Wing commander A. C. P. Carver with Wing Commander Henri de Rancourt as French Commandant, was re-formed at West Raynham with Douglas Havocs and Bostons crewed mainly by Free French Air Force officers who had resided at Sculthorpe since January. 'A' Flight was known as Metz Flight and 'B' Flight was called Nancy Flight. No.342 'Lorraine' Squadron was working up on the Boston IIIA at Sculthorpe. The Free French Boston IIIAs were in short supply so training was carried out on early Bostons and some Havoc Is and IIs. The need to lay concrete runways at West Raynham in May led to the French having to move to Sculthorpe. No.342 'Lorraine' Squadron flew its first Boston operation on 12 June with an attack on the power station at Rouen.

During April and May the squadron underwent intensive training, moving to Sculthorpe on 15 May. Four days later 1482 (B) G Flight moved to Great Massingham with Mitchells, Venturas and Martinets. The station then closed down for concrete runways and perimeter track to be laid. The boundaries to the west were extended to accommodate two new hard runways, one at 2,000 yards in length and one at 1,400 yards, and perimeter track. The runways were completed by November 1943. During the construction programme by Allot Ltd fourteen loop-type standings were added to take the final number to thirty-seven and increased accommodation could now cater for 2,456 airmen and 658 WAAFs. The Martinet target tugs were detached here from 15 July 1943 followed by the Mitchells and Venturas in September. The following month a few Hurricanes were added to the flight, which moved to Swanton Morley on 2 December 1943.

No.100 (Bomber Support) Group took over the station on 3 December 1943 and operated Mosquitoes until the end of the war. Bomber Command operations carried out from this station during the war claimed eighty-six aircraft: fifty-six Blenheims, twenty-nine Mosquitoes and a Beaufighter.

The last unit to be stationed at Raynham was 66 Squadron, which was equipped with Rapier missiles and which completed a tour of duty in the Gulf War, defending Bahrain International

Airport against air attack. The station closed on 1 June 1994. (*See also Great Massingham and Weasenham Hall.*)

WEYBOURNE

From the mid-1930s the army used the coastal airfield at Weybourne for summer anti-aircraft gunnery practice camps. Target-tug aircraft stationed at Bircham Newton towed sleeve targets for the gunners to fire at. In the early days the tugs were Westland Wallaces of the AACU. By 1939 these were replaced by Hawker Henleys. A large field adjoining the site was used as a landing ground. On 26 July 1938 Wallace K8678 of 1 AACU crashed while on approach to Weybourne. In 1939 a catapult was built atop the cliff and on 16 May 'X' Flight of the AACU arrived from Henlow with de Havilland Queen Bee target drones (radio-controlled seaplane and landplane versions of the Tiger Moth). These were launched by catapult and flown along the coast at various heights while the gunners fired at them. Those that survived were landed on the sea and picked up by tender, or in the case of the landplanes, were brought back to the landing strip. On 12 September 1939 'X' Flight moved to Watchet.

In January and February 1941 a hangar and several wooden buildings were constructed for 'T' Flight AACU, which arrived from Farnborough on 3 February 1941 with Queen Bees. Officers were billeted at Carvel farmhouse while the other ranks lived in wooden huts which also accommodated the NAAFI and MT section etc. On the night of 24/25 May 1941 a Heinkel He 111 dropped a stick of four 250 kg UXBs across the site.

From June 1941 the drones were used as targets for the new rocket projectiles. Visitors who observed the rocket-firing demonstrations included the AOC 70 Group, Air Commodore Cole-Hamilton and the Prime Minister, Winston Churchill. Other weapons used included Bofors light anti-aircraft, guns. 'T' Flight disbanded at Weybourne on 29 April 1942 and by July flying at the station had ended, although the anti-aircraft (AA) camp remained.

After the war Weybourne was renamed No.1 Anti-Aircraft Practice Camp. British pilotless target aircraft (PTAs) were launched from inside the camp and were recovered by parachute. When Stiffkey AA Camp closed, Weybourne assumed all Light Anti-Aircraft (LAA) gunnery in addition to medium and heavy

AA gunnery. Site facilities were also provided for US Army anti-aircraft artillery (AAA) practice firing using Skysweeper AA guns, which had fire-control radar mounted on the gun platform. Truck-mounted multiple 0.5 calibre machine guns were also used. The Americans provided their own PTAs, which were considerably faster than the British version, and again they were launched by catapult with parachute recovery. Sleeve targets were towed mainly by Beaufighter TT.10 and Mosquito TT.35 aircraft of No.2 CAACU at Langham until the site finally closed in 1958.

SUMMARY OF THE AIRFIELDS AND LOCATIONS

Attlebridge

Description: RAF medium bomber station prior to US 8th Air Force use.

Location: in the parish of Werston Longville about 8 miles north-west of Norwich.

Directions: Follow the A47 Norwich–Dereham road to Weston Longville.

Comments: Now a turkey farm. Some wartime huts and watch office in evidence.

Unit	From/To	Aircraft
105 Sqn	June 1941	Blenheim IV
320 (Dutch) Sqn	30 March–30 August 1943	Mitchell II
1508 Flt	4 April–29 August 1943	Oxford
88 Sqn	1 August 1941–29 Sept 1942	Blenheim IV/Boston III
247 Sqn	7–13 August 1943	Typhoon I

Barton Bendish

Description: satellite for RAF Marham

Location: A short distance south of Barton Bendish village, which is about 3 miles from Marham airfield.

Comments: The site of the landing ground can still be seen as a series of large fields with an absence of large trees or hedges.

Unit	From/To	Aircraft
38/115/218 Sqns	September 1939–	Wellington
56 OTU Unit	early part of the war	Hurricane
New Zealand Flt	early 1940–	Wellington
268 (Army Co-Op) Sqn det.	September–October 1941	Tomahawk IIa/ Lysander III
26 (Army Co-Op) Sqn det.	November 1941	Tomahawk IIa/ Lysander III
218 CF	1942	Wellington/Stirling

Bircham Newton

Description: Operational RAF and FAA aerodrome 1916–1948. RAF Technical Training Command from October 1948 to December 1962. In 1954 the airfield was deemed no longer required.

Location: 8 miles from Fakenham.

Comments: Since 1966 Bircham has become the site of the National Construction College (East). A heritage centre off the main road contains memorabilia relating to the RAF station history. Nearby are two stone tablets in memory of those who served at Bircham 1917–62 and squash courts that are reputed to be haunted with ghosts of a Wellington crew that took off one night, hit a church and as agreed met up again in the squash courts.

At Great Bircham cemetery about 1 mile south-west of Bircham Newton are the graves of thirty-seven RAF, seventeen RCAF, four RAAF, six RNZAF and eleven *Luftwaffe* airmen.

Unit	From/To	Aircraft
206 Sqn	June 1936–July 1941	Anson GR.I/ Hudson I/II/III/IV
220 Sqn	17 Aug 1936–21 Aug 1939	Anson
42 Sqn	18 Aug 1939–28 Apr 1940	Vildebeest
48 Sqn det	Aug 1939–Jul 1940	Anson
233 Sqn det	Oct 1939–Aug 1940	Blenheim
254 Sqn	28 Jan–24 Apr 1940	Blenheim

2 GRU	4 March–16 May 1940	Wellington
235 Sqn	25 Apr–26 May 1940	Blenheim
235 Sqn	24 Jun 1940–4 Jun 1941	Blenheim
59 Sqn det	Jul 1940–Jun 1941	Hudson
1403 Flt	Nov 1940–7 Feb 1942	Blenheim/Hudson
221 Sqn	21 Nov 1940–29 Sep 1941	Wellington
252 Sqn	21 Nov–1 Dec 1940	Blenheim
53 Sqn	Jul 1940–20 Oct 1941	Blenheim
200 Sqn	25 May–18 Jun 1941	Hudson
500 Sqn	30 May 1941–22 Mar 1942	Blenheim/Hudson
248 Sqn	15 Jun 1941–17 Feb 1942	Blenheim/Beaufighter
1401 Flt	25 Oct 1941–1 Aug 1942	
279 Sqn	16 Nov 1941–31 Oct 1944	Hudson
280 Sqn	10 Feb 1942–25 Sep 1943	Anson
407 Sqn	31 Mar–1 Oct 1942	Hudson
320 (Dutch) Sqn	21 Apr 1942–15 Mar 1943	Hudson
1525 Flt	13 Jul 1942–26 Jun 1945	Oxford
521 Sqn	22 Jul 1942–22 Mar 1943	Blenheim/Spitfire/ Mosquito/Hudson/ Gladiator
1611 Flt	9 Nov 1942–1 Dec 1943	Henley
1612 Flt	8 Dec 1942–1 Dec 1943	Henley
53 Sqn	18 March–29 Apr 1943	Hudson/Whitley
2 ATC	16 June 1943–July 1945	
415 Sqn	15 Nov 1943–26 Jul 1944	Wellington/Albacore
ASRTU	13–20 Oct 1943	Wellington/ Warwick ASR.I/ Sea Otter
Warwick TU	3 July–13 Oct 1943	Warwick ASR.I/ Wellington
1626 Flt	30 Nov–1 Dec 1943	Lysander
695 Sqn	1 Dec 1943–11 Aug 1945	Henley III/Hurricane IIc/ Vengeance IV/ Martinet I/Lysander I and II
524 Sqn	23 July–17 Oct 1944	Wellington

48 Sqn det	21–23 Feb 1944	Beaufighter
CCPP	June 1944–late–1945	Mosquito/Beaufighter/ Wellington/Albacore
855 Sqn FAA	7–14 Sep 1944	Avenger
819 Sqn FAA	1 Oct–1 Nov 1944	Swordfish
119 Sqn	2 Oct 1944–21 Feb 1945	Albacore
819 Sqn FAA	26 Feb–10 Mar 1945	Swordfish
598 Sqn	12 Mar–30 Apr 1945	Hurricane/Oxford/ Martinet/Beaufighter
119 Sqn	22 May 1945	Albacore

Blickling Hall,
Norwich NR11 6NF (tel 01263 733084 Fax 734924.)

The 'three Ms' – Sergeant Jim 'Dinty' Moore, Pilot Officer George W. Milson and Sergeant Ron Millar RNZAF – in the gardens of Blickling Hall in June 1941. (*Jim Moore*)

Description: Mess for 2 Group and 100 Group personnel in the Second World War.

Location: 1 mile west of Aylsham on B1354 Aylsham to Saxthorpe road signposted off the A140 Cromer Road.

Directions: If visiting Oulton, carry on through the village past the memorial to the first T-junction and turn right along the B1354 Aylsham – Saxthorpe road. From Aylsham, head along the B1354 towards Saxthorpe. Blickling Hall is on the right.

Comments: Whether you are an aviation enthusiast or not, no visit to Norfolk is complete without a visit to one of the greatest houses in East Anglia which during the war was an RAF officers' mess, evidence of which can still be seen. The National Trust has arranged an exhibition in the barn at the visitor's car park of the Hall to describe the RAF use of Oulton and the Hall.

Jack Peppiatt, an 88 Squadron Boston pilot at Oulton was at

Blickling from September 1942 to the summer of 1943.

It was a most wonderful period on several levels; high drama in terms of the war and the seductive delights of a country mansion during the quiet moments. We had visits from ENSA troupes who performed in a barn near the house; elegant evenings with all present to see people like Reg Dixon and Tessie O'Shea. Afterwards they were invited into either the sergeants' or officers' mess. On one visit Tessie came with her pianist and manager to our anti-room after a tiring day of travel and performing. The beautiful room was crowded with RAF and invited visitors from local forces units. As usual she was being asked to do a song for us as a favour, but Tessie wasn't the favouring kind in private life I fear. She refused briskly but after a lot of, slightly drunken, prodding she agreed with poor grace to do just one. She set off; the room was packed as people pushed in to get a view. Then, in the distance, the skirl of the pipes, and into the room marched two burly pipers from the Black Watch, having been told in their innocence to do so by a troublemaker. Tessie O'Shea's response was several four-letter words, which in those days were not often heard, in mixed company.

For a period of two or three weeks the squadron moved down to a forward airfield leaving three or four crews to hold the fort at Blickling. We lucky ones lived the life of Riley, we fished in the lake, poached game and every evening we had a banquet. We roamed the house looking at the treasures that were still tucked away. At Christmas 1942 we had a wonderful party in the dining room; stuffed pike and even swan. There was great competition to secure the affections of the local vicar's niece (I believe).

A popular bit of fun so thought, was to carry a Very cartridge into the dining room, surreptitiously held behind the back, stand before the ornate fireplace until the chosen victim was eating and then toss it into the fire and walk smartly out. The room would fill up to neck level with black smoke. This became less popular after someone did it whilst the CO was having his breakfast.

I suppose because of the splendour of the surroundings we all tried to live up to them and evening dinner was a well-dressed performance; however the usual behaviour always followed. I can clearly see us all seated in the small, first anteroom, around the walls. The door to the dining-room was open and the floor cleared on our side, but with a beer mug on the carpet behind a table. The idea was to gain speed in the dining room, dive through the door over the table and do a forward roll placing the head in the mug on landing. Participants removed tunics and ties ... this whole process was carried out in a decorous way with the CO commenting on style and content of performance.

Bodney

Description: Satellite airfield and USAAF fighter base July 1942–November 1945.

Location: 4½ miles from Watton.

Directions: Take the B1108 south-east of Hillborough.

Comments: Long since MoD property within the Stanford Training Area and a British Army camp. One of the control towers (there were two but a Mustang crashed into one of them) remains. There is no memorial to RAF crews but next to the main gate of the army barracks is a memorial stone to the 352nd Fighter Group, dedicated on 9 July 1983.

Unit	From/To	Aircraft
21 Sqn det	Sep 1939–Dec 1941	Blenheim IV
82 Sqn	1 Oct 1940–18 Apr 1941	Blenheim IV
90 Sqn	May 1941	Fortress I
105 Sqn	21 May–July 1941	Blenheim IV
82 Sqn	3 May–11 June 1941	Blenheim IV
17 (P) AFU	29 Jan 1942–1 May 1943	Master/Anson
21 Sqn	14 March–30 Oct 1942	Blenheim IV/Ventura /II
352nd FG (328th/486th/ 487thFS)	7 July 43–3 Nov 45	P-47D/P-38/P-51C/D/K

Coltishall

Description: RAF fighter station Second World War to 2006.

Location: 9 miles north-north-east of Norwich.

Directions: follow the B1150 from Norwich.

Comments: At the former RAF Coltishall there are six cherry trees planted and dedicated in memory of six airmen killed in a coach crash when 41 Squadron was detached to West Germany. A cairn with an inscribed plaque giving details of date and airmen killed on 21 May 1983 was relocated to the Scattow Cemetry shortly before the closure of RAF Coltishall on 30 November 2006. At the entrance of the former amenities centre, a plaque is inscribed: 'The centre was opened by HRH the Princess Royal'.

At Douglas Bader Close in North Walsham on the town's industrial estate is a plaque dedicated to the memory of Douglas Bader which was named in a ceremony on 9 June 1989 by Lady Bader. (*See also Horning, Scottow and Stratton Strawless.*)

Unit	From/To	Aircraft
66 Sqn	29 May–3 Sep 1940	Spitfire I
242 Sqn	18 Jun–26 Oct 1940	Hurricane I
616 Sqn AAF	3–9 September 1940	Spitfire I
604 Sqn det	July 1940–21 Sept 1941	Blenheim I/Beaufighter I
74 Sqn	9 Sep–15 Oct 1940	Spitfire I/IIa
72 Sqn	13 Oct–30 Oct 1940	Spitfire I
64 Sqn	15 Oct–10 Nov 1940	Spitfire I
72 Sqn	2–29 Nov 1940	Spitfire I
222 Sqn	11 Nov 1940–6 June 1941	Spitfire I/IIa
242 Sqn	30 Nov–16 Dec 1940	Hurricane I
257 Sqn	17 Dec 1940–7 Nov 1941	Hurricane I/IIa/IIc
93 Sqn det	Dec 1940–Nov 1941	Havoc I
42 Sqn det	March 1941–June 1942	Beaufort I/II
2 ADF	18 March 1941–23 July 1943	
151 Sqn det	22 April 1941–3 May 1941	Hurricane I/Defiant I

29 Sqn det	April 1941–May 1943	Beaufighter I/VI
151 Sqn det	21 May 1941–25 Jan 1942	Hurricane I/IIb/IIc/Defiant I
133 Sqn	1–15 Aug 1941	Hurricane IIb
12 Gp TTF	August–8 December 1941	Lysander II/III
255 Sqn	20 September 1941–2 Mar 1942	Beaufighter IIf
288 Sqn det	Nov 1941	Blenheim IV/Hurricane I/II/Lysander II/III
137 Sqn	8 Nov–1 December 1941	Whirlwind I
1489 TTF (12 Grp)	8 Dec 1941–May 1942	Lysander II/III/IIIa/Henley III
152 Sqn	1 Dec 1941–17 Jan 1942	Spitfire IIa
266 Sqn det	Jan–Aug 1942	Spitfire Vb/Typhoon Ia/Ib
68 Sqn	8 Mar 1942–5 Feb 1944	Beaufighter I/VI
154 Sqn	17 March–May 1942	Spitfire Va/Vb
278 Sqn	10 Apr 1942–30 Apr 1944	Anson I/Lysander IIIa/Walrus I/II
1489 (Fighter) GF	May–December 1942	Lysander II/III/IIIa/Henley III/Master I
488 Sqn det	Sep 1942–August 1943	Beaufighter II/VI
346th FS USAAF	Nov 1942–3 June 1943	P-400/Spitfire V
118 Sqn	17 Jan–15 Aug 1943	Spitfire V
288 Sqn det	Jan 1943–Nov 1944	Defiant I/II/Oxford I/II/Beaufighter I/Spit V/IX
841 Sqn FAA Det	7 Feb–23 June 1943	Albacore I/Swordfish I/II
409 Sqn det	Feb 1943–May 1944	Beaufighter I/Mosquito XIII
613 Sqn Det	3–27 May 1943	Mustang I
FIU	June 1943–March 1944	Havoc I/Welkin I/Mosquito VI/XII/XVII/Beaufighter VIf/Hurricane IIC/Tempest V
611 Sqn	4 Aug 1943–8 Feb 1944	Spitfire Vb/Vc/IX
151 Sqn det	Aug 1943–Mar 1944	Mosquito
195 Sqn	21 August–21 Sep 1943	Typhoon Ib

64 Sqn	25 Sep 1943–21 Jan 1944	Spitfire Vb
234 Sqn	28 Jan–18 Mar 1944	Spitfire Vb/Vc
64 Sqn	3 Feb–April 1944	Spitfire Vb
316 (Polish) Sqn	28 Feb–4 July 1944	Mustang III
25 Sqn	5 Feb–27 Oct 1944	Mosquito VI/XVII
307 (Polish) Sqn	1 May 1944–30 Jan 1945	Beaufighter VI/ Mosquito XI/XII/XXX
229 Sqn	1 July–25 Sep 1944	Spitfire IX
312 (Czech) Sqn	11 July–27 August 1944	Spitfire IX
316 (Polish) Sqn	28 August–24 Oct 1944	Mustang III
NFDU	Sept 1944–May 1945	various
80 Sqn	20-29 Sep 1944	Spitfire
274 Sqn	20-29 Sep 1944	Tempest
303 (Polish) Sqn	25 Sep 1944–4 April 1945	Spitfire
453 Sqn RAAF	30 Sep–18 Oct 1944	Spitfire IX
602 Sqn AAF	30 Sep–18 Oct 1944	Spitfire IX
125 Sqn	18 Oct 1944–24 Apr 1945	Mosquito
315 (Polish) Sqn	24 Oct–1 Nov 1944	Spitfire
68 Sqn	28 Oct 1944–16 Mar 1945	Beaufighter
229 Sqn	1 July–25 Sept 1944	Spitfire IX
229 Sqn	2 Dec 1944–10 Jan 1945	Spitfire
603 Sqn AAF	10 Jan–24 Feb 1945	Spitfire
26 Sqn det	Jan–Apr 1945	Mustang
124 Sqn	10 Feb–7 Apr 1945	Spitfire
603 Sqn AAF	5–28 Apr 1945	Spitfire
1 Sqn	8 Apr 1945–14 May 1945	Spitfire
602 Sqn	9 Apr–15 May 1945	Spitfire
316 (Polish) Sqn	6 May–10 Aug 1945	Mustang
303 (Polish) Sqn	16 May–10 August 1945	Mustang
215 Sqn	8 Aug 1945–14 Jan 1947	Spitfire
306 (Polish) Sqn	10 Aug 1945–6 Jan 1947	Mustang
309 (Polish) Sqn	10 Aug 1945–6 Jan 1947	Mustang

Docking

Description: Decoy site, relief landing ground and satellite airfield for Bircham Newton.

Location: 10 miles north-east of Fakenham.

Directions: East of B1153 from Docking village.

Comments: The airfield has returned to agriculture and most of the buildings are on private land. The eastern section of the perimeter track survives and along the southern edge the control tower can be seen.

Unit	From/To	Aircraft
812 Sqn FAA	Spring 1940	Swordfish
1403 Met Flt	Spring 1940	Blenheim
235 Sqn	July 1940–June 1941	Blenheim
206 Sqn	September 1940	Hudson I
1401 (Met) Flt	March 1941–July 1942	Blenheim/Hurricane/Spitfire/Gladiator
53 Sqn	July–October 1941	Blenheim IV
225 Sqn	July 1941–August 1942	Lysander III/Hurricane I/II/Mustang I
241 Sqn	August 1941	Tomahawk II
22/1522 BAT Flt	October 1941–April 1942	Oxford I
288 Sqn	July 1941–August 1942	Hudson GRIII/Oxford II/Defiant I/Lysander I/II/Hurricane I
221 Sqn	25 December 1941–8 Jan 1942	Wellington Ic/VIII
502 Sqn	12 January–22 February 1942	Whitley V/VII
235 Sqn	31 May–16 July 1942	Beaufighter Ic
143 Sqn	27 July–27 August 1942	Blenheim IVc/Beaufighter Ic
254 Sqn	10 October–7 November 1942	Beaufighter VIf
2 APC	November 1942–February 1945	Martinet
407 Sqn	10 Nov 1942–16 Feb 1943	Hudson V/Wellington XI
53 Sqn	February–April 1943	Whitley VII

415 Sqn	February–May 1943	Hampden
304 Sqn	2 April–7 Jun 1943	Wellington Ic/X
1525 BAT Flt	April 1943–July 1945	Oxford I
1401 (Met) Flt	April–1 Sept 1943	Gladiator II
Warwick TU	28 June–3 July 1943	Warwick ASR.I
519 Sqn	August–December 1943	Ventura V
521 Sqn	1 Sep 1943–30 October 1944	Hampden I/Hudson III/ Ventura/ Gladiator II/ Spitfire IX/Mentor/ Tiger Moth
415 Sqn	November 1943–July 1944	Wellington XIII
288 Sqn	November 1943–July 1944	Oxford II/Martinet
855 Sqn FAA	May–October 1944	Avenger I
524 Sqn	May–October 1944	Wellington XIV
288 Sqn	May–July 1945	Oxford II
1693 Flt	31 May–11 August 1945	Wellington III/ Warwick ASR.I

Downham Market

Description: RAF bomber station.

Location: 2 miles north-east of Downham Market and east of A10.

Directions: Follow the A10 between Bexwell and Stow Bardolph and look for the large radio masts that denote the eastern and western extremities of the site.

Comments: After the war the airfield was used by light aircraft and crop-sprayers until the late 1970s. In the early 1980s the remaining concrete was broken up and used for the eastern bypass around the town. The A10 follows approximately the line of the former north-east–south-west runway and just before the Bexwell roundabout passes a short section of concrete to the east that is the only remaining part of the main east–west runway. The third runway, which ran north-west–south-east, has been removed but much of the perimeter track survives – the western section is now a public footpath. The technical site is an industrial

133

estate and many of the wartime buildings have been modified for use; For example, the former Guardroom is now a kitchen showroom. Inside Bexwell church is a memorial tablet to 214, 218, 608, 623 and 635 Squadrons. The VC memorial in the churchyard includes detailed inscriptions of the two actions concerning Flight Sergeant Arthur Louis Aaron DFM, pilot of a 218 Stirling on 12/13 August 1943 and Acting Squadron Leader Ian Willoughby Bazalgette DFC RAFVR 'master bomber' of a 635 Squadron Lancaster on 4 August 1944. Eight RAF personnel of two world wars are buried in the cemetery. They include three RAFVR airmen of 635 Squadron who died when Lancaster ND841 flew into a hangar at Downham Market and exploded. A housing estate on the site of the old aerodrome has roads called Stirling Close and Lancaster Crescent. Nearby is Airfield Farm.

On Sunday 4 November 1990 a memorial plaque in All Saints Church, Bawdeswell just off the A47 was dedicated to Pilot Officer James McLean (twenty-six) and Sergeant Mervyn Tansley (twenty-one) of 608 (North Riding) Squadron, who died when their Mosquito hit the church returning from Gelsenkirchen on 6 November 1944. The twelve Mosquito BXXs of the squadron began returning over Norfolk shortly before 2100 hours to Downham Market. They had to contend with cloud and icing conditions as they descended over the flat landscape. The Mosquito flown by McLean began to ice up badly and he lost control during his descent through cloud. The Mosquito struck overhead electric power cables before crashing into the village church. Both whirling propellers sheered off the engine nacelles and fell into neighbouring gardens, where a tree was cut down as if hit by a chainsaw. The remains of McLean and Tansley were not recovered from the wreckage until nine days later.

Unit	From/To	Aircraft
214 Sqn	10 Dec 1943–16 Jan 1944	Stirling I/III
218 Sqn	7 July 1942–7 March 1944	Stirling I/III
571 Sqn	7–22 April 1944	Mosquito B.XVI
608 Sqn	1 August 1944–28 August 1945	Mosquito B.XX/B.XVI/B.XXV
623 Sqn	10 August–6 December 1943	Stirling III
635 Sqn	20 Mar 1944–1 Sep 1945	Lancaster I/III/VI

East Wretham

Description: Satellite for RAF Honington and from October 1943 to November 1945 base for the 359th FG US 8th AF.

Location: On Breckland Heath 5 miles north-east of Thetford and south-west of East Wretham village.

Directions: Follow the A47 Norwich–Dereham road to Weston Longville and on to the A1075.

Comments: Now an army camp within the Stanford Training Area. some wartime buildings remain. In the Commonwealth airmen's section in St Ethelbert's churchyard twelve Czechoslovakian RAFVR airmen are buried, including Leading Aircraft man Jan Bambusek (twenty-eight, 4 April 1942), Sergeant Frantisek Binder (twenty-seven, 4 March 1942). Three Czechs – Sergeants Frantisek Desek and Maxmilian Stocek and Pilot Officer Stanislav Zeinert died in the crash of a 311 Squadron Wellington when it stalled on take-off from Langham on 26 May 1941. Sergeants Rudolf Grimm, Jindrich Horinek, Aldis Keda and Rudolf Vokurka, F/Sgt Jan Stanovsky and P/O Jan Stefek were killed on 6 April 1942 when Wellington P9299 of the Czech OTF crashed in poor visibility near Ilanymawddwy, Merionthshire. Pilot Officer Miloslav Svic died on 4 June 1941.

At the village war memorial near the church is a small metal plaque inscribed: 'This plaque commemorates the visit by survivors of the 359th Fighter Group, in remembrance of those who served and died in the cause of freedom, 3 August 1985.' The 359th Fighter Group were based at East Wretham in 1944-45.

In Thetford on the wall of the old library in Guildhall Street is a plaque: 'In memory of 311 (Czechoslovak) Squadron, RAF which operated from RAF Honington and East Wretham and its 273 members who lost their lives in the fight for freedom 1940-1945, placed here by free Czechoslovakian airmen 1980.' Outside the council offices is a stone memorial: 'Presented to the people of Thetford and East Wretham, a memorial honouring the men of the 359th Fighter Group who gave their lives and those who also served during WWII. 67th Fighter Wing, US 8th Air Force, East Wretham and Great Hockham, airfield 133 1943–1945. Dedicated 3rd August 1985.'

In Thetford also is the Dad's Army Trail, named after the

famous BBC TV series, which can be walked and takes about an hour. The route goes past locations where the series was filmed. (The opening sequence and many scenes used in the series were filmed at Stanford Battle Area nearby). From the Bell Hotel in Bridge Street, where the cast and crew stayed during filming, to the Guildhall, where the whole unit once stood on parade, there are enough sites of interest to keep any fan happy. (Tel. Thetford Tourism on 01842 820689)

Unit	From/To	Aircraft
311 Czech Sqn	16 Sept 1940–28 April 1942	Wellington Ia/Ic
CTU/1429 Flt	1 January–26 June 1942	Wellington Ic/Oxford I
115 Sqn	8 Nov–1942–6 August 1943	Wellington III/ Lancaster II
1678 HCU	18 May–6 August 1943	Lancaster II

Feltwell

Description: RAF bomber airfield in the Second World War now Space Command's 5th Space Surveillance Squadron, USAF.

Location: 5 miles from Brandon, to the left of the B1112.

Directions: Turn left in Feltwell village.

Comments: Used by the US Space Command's 5th Space Surveillance Squadron, one of the airfield's most noticeable features are the white 'golf balls' which house surveillance equipment. Wartime hangars and most original buildings remain, long since converted for USAF use.

Unit	From/To	Aircraft
214 Sqn	12 April 1937–3 Sep 1939	Harrow/Wellington
New Zealand Flt	12 February–4 April 1940	
75 Sqn RNZAF	4 April 1940–15 Aug 1942	Wellington
57 Sqn	20 November 1940–5 Jan 1942	Wellington
BCSMS	3 Jan 1941–30 November 1942	
1519 Flt	December 1941–3 Jul 1945	Oxford
487 Sqn RNZAF	15 Aug 1942–3 April 1943	Ventura

464 Sqn RAAF	1 Sep 1942–3 April 1943	Ventura
192 Sqn	5 April–25 November 1943	Halifax/Mosquito/ Wellington
BDU	6 April–13 Sep 1943	Lancaster III/ Warwick ASRI/ Halifax III/Fortress III
1473 Flt	14 Sep–28 November 1943	Anson/Wellington
3 LFS	21 Nov 1943–31 Jan 1945	Lancaster
G-H TF	29 December 1944–5 Jun 1945	Lancaster I/III
BDU	7 Dec 1943–25 Feb 1945	Lancaster III/ Warwick ASR.I/ Halifax III/Fortress III/ Auster AOP.V/Lincoln I
BCRS	29 December 1944–Sep 1946	
1688 Flt	25 February 1945–19 Mar 1946	Lancaster/Spitfire/ Hurricane

Fersfield

Description: 2 Group RAF, and USAAF bomber airfield.

Location: 4 miles north-east of South Lopham.

Directions: Follow the A1066 west from Diss.

Comments: Little trace of the airfield remains; only a few crumbling wartime buildings are in evidence. In Fersfield churchyard is a memorial to the airmen stationed at the airfield in the Second World War. Nearby is Bressingham Steam Museum and Gardens where the locomotive *Royal Scot* can be seen.

Unit	From/To	Aircraft
USAAF Aphrodite/Anvil Projects	12 July 1944–1 January 1945	B-17/PB4Y-1 drones/ B.34 Ventura
2 Group TF/SU	Dec 1944–31 Dec 1945	aircrew training/ aircrew & gunnery training
180 Sqn	7–14 June 1945	Mosquito FBVI
107 Sqn	3–10 July 1945	Mosquito FBVI
140 Sqn	9–12 July 1945	Mosquito FBVI

Foulsham

Description: Light bomber, heavy bomber and 100 Group airfield in the Second World War.

Location: 15 miles north-west of Norwich in the parishes of Wood Norton and Foulsham and a half mile north of Foulsham village.

Directions: follow the A1067 Norwich – Fakenham road and turn right just after the water tower to your left. Drive on through Foulsham village, stopping to inspect the village sign with its reference to the local airfield and head towards Hindolveston taking great care on the winding, twisting road. The airfield buildings that remain are on your left.

Comments: Three hangars remain intact and between them are several buildings, either disused or in use by local industry. Above the doorway of one of the buildings is painted, 'Ground Equipment'.

Unit	From/To	Aircraft
98 Sqn	15 Oct 1942–18 August 1943	Mitchell II
180 Sqn	19 Oct 1942–18 August 1943	Mitchell II
375th SS USAAF	October 1943–Feb 1944	Mosquito F8
192 Squadron	October 1943–Feb 1944	Halifax II/III/V/ Mosquito IV/XVI/ Anson I/Wellington X
1473 Flight	December 1943–February 1944	Wellington III/Anson I
BSDU	May 1944–20 Dec 1944	Mosquito FBVI/NFXIX
7th Photo Group USAAF	August 1944–March 1945	P-38J (F-5) Lightning
171 Squadron	September–October 1944	Stirling III/Halifax III
462 RAAF Sqn	December 1944–Sept 1945	Halifax III
199 Squadron	July 1945–June 1946	Halifax III

Great Massingham

Description: Light bomber, day bomber and 100 Group night intruder airfield in the Second World War.

Location: 2 miles from West Raynham on a site directly adjacent to Great Massingham village.

Directions: Great Massingham can be reached via the Bawdeswell – Kings Lynn (B1145) road, branching off right just after crossing the A1065 Swaffham – Fakenham Road.

Comments: Great Massingham is a picturesque village with a large pond and delightful little shops. Now a private airfield, the former station is easily accessible, as part of the perimeter track is a public footpath, but apart form the runways only a single T2 hangar remains. On the western side of the village there is a water tower and a well-preserved RAF gymnasium. The Fox and Pheasant and Royal Oak, popular wartime pubs in Great Massingham, are now private residences.

Leaving the village and heading for the A148 Fakenham – King's Lynn road, make an immediate turn left to the churchyard of St Andrew, Little Massingham where there are seven RAF graves in the graveyard. Squadron Leader Hugh J. N. Lindsaye died on 30 April 1941, the pilot of an 18 Squadron Blenheim IV (V6389) on a drogue-towing practice, testing the drogue (sleeve) when it separated from the cable; the cable fouled the port tailplane. The Blenheim dived into a field at Hillington and was destroyed. Sergeant A. E. Stone, observer, is buried at Scarborough and Flying Officer F. Holmes, air gunner at Marham (Holy Trinity). Other graves include Sergeant J. C. Wilson RNZAF, 21 May 1941 (twenty-seven) 107 Squadron; Sergeant John C. 'Polly' Weston, who was Sergeant Kenneth Wolstenholme's observer and was killed when their Blenheim was hit by flak on an operation to Heligoland, Sergeant T. P. P. Poole, 19 February 1942 (twenty-six) 107 Squadron, who was the observer on Boston III W8319 which crashed into ground on take-off at Little Massingham with all crew killed; Pilot Officer A. E. Lockwood, 1 April 1942 (twenty-two) 107 Squadron, who was the pilot of Boston III AL264 which crashed near Great Massingham – the rest of the crew survived; Flight Sergeant G. T. Relph, 27 August 1942 (twenty-four) 107 Squadron, the observer on Boston III AL715, which ditched in the sea after an attack on the aerodrome at Abbeville in daylight – the rest of the crew were injured but survived. Flying Officer C. S. Ronayne, 11 June 1944 (thirty-three), 141 Squadron, the navigator of Mosquito II HJ916 from West Raynham, which crashed at Newmarket due to the structural failure of the port wing and the pilot baled out. Flying Officer J. R. Watkins, 1 January 1945 (twenty-one), 239 Squadron, the navigator on Mosquito FBVI PZ340 from West Raynham, which was diverted due to mist and crashed at Narford Hall near Downham Market. It was presumed that there had been loss of control on the instruments. The pilot, Flying Officer Walker, was also killed.

Returning to the main road, turn left and a few hundred yards further on to the left back from the road is the religious retreat which in the Second World War was a manor house requisitioned as a mess by RAF units at Massingham.

Unit	From/To	Aircraft
18 Sqn	8 Sep 1940–3 April 1941	Blenheim IV
90 Sqn	15 May–August 1941	Fortress I
107 Sqn	11 May 1941–20 August 1943	Blenheim IV
342 'Lorraine' Sqn	19 July–6 Sep 1943	Boston IIIa
1692 Flt	21 May 1944–16 June 1945	Anson I/Mosquito FBVI/ NFXIX/TIII/ BeaufighterVf/ Wellington XVIII/ Oxford II
1694 Bomber Defence Training Flight	April 1944–30 July 1945	Spitfire/Martinet TT.1
169 Sqn	4 June 1944–10 August 1945	Mosquito FBVI/NFXIX
1692 Bomber Support	17 June 1944–16 August 1945	Mosquito FBVI/NFXIX/ TIII/Beaufighter Vf/ Wellington
Training Unit		XVIII/Anson I/Oxford II
CFE	October 1944–August 1945	Mosquito/Spitfire/ Tempest II
1482 Flt	29 May 1943–17 Sep 1943	Lysander/Blenheim/ Defiant

Horning

Description: Beautiful Broadland village with pubs and river frequented in wartime by airmen from RAF Coltishall.

Location: On the A1062 Coltishall – Ludham road opposite the turn for RAF Neatishead radar station.

Directions: Take the A1151 from Norwich to Wroxham, where a right turn is made onto the A1062.

Comments: On a dark, moonless night, Saturday 26 April 1941 at 21.45 hours a Junkers Ju 88 flying at 500 feet dropped fifteen bombs in the vicinity of the Ferry Inn. The Inn seems an unlikely target but when war broke out in 1939 the firm of H. C. Banham Ltd started Admiralty work on 27-foot whalers. Then they co-operated for war production with the Percival firm and joined in the construction of motor launches, motor torpedo boats and invasion craft generally until the end of 1944 when the building of the larger ships was drawing to a close. The Fairmile Marine Company delivered 1,500 tons of ships of war fully equipped for action, mainly for the navy but also for the RAF. One of the RAF's favourite drinking haunts was the Ferry Inn, which stood quite on its own in open country. Pilots from all the Coltishall squadrons nearby were in there three or four evenings a week. The bulk of the bombs fell aimlessly on the surrounding marshland. Four fell on the Ferry Inn property, one dropped on the pontoon ferryboat, ten on the Woodbastwick side of the river and one in the river itself. The second of the series of bombs hit the public house, killing twenty-one people and injuring several

The Ferry Inn public house at the furthermost end of Horning village where on 26 April 1941 a bomb dropped by a Ju 88 flying at 500 feet killed twenty-one people including three RAF Coltishall airmen, one of whom was Robinson, the 222 Squadron adjutant. Another was one of their pilots, South African Flight Lieutenant Brian van Mentz DFC and the third was Attwell, the Coltishall Station Medical Officer. (*Author*)

more. Of six members of the family of Mr Henry Sutton, a well-known figure in the Yarmouth fishing trade, five were killed, including Mr Sutton himself. The landlord, Albert Stringer, and about half a dozen others were dug out alive, though most of them were seriously injured. Rescue squads came from Aylsham and Sprowston, and their efforts were supplemented by troops stationed locally. On the Sunday 'Lord Haw-Haw' gloated on the wireless over this triumph for the German war machine, and gleefully announced that an establishment on the Broads for building warships had been successfully raided from the air.

Among the RAF dead was Robinson, 222 Squadron's adjutant, one of their pilots, South African Flight Lieutenant Brian van Mentz DFC (who had seven victories and one shared) and Attwell, the Coltishall Station Medical Officer. Squadron Leader Robert Stanford Tuck DSO DFC**, CO of 257 'Burma' Squadron at Coltishall and his fiancée Joyce, whom he had met recently in the upstairs bar of the King's Arms in North Walsham, escaped death or injury by leaving early. Tuck said that all at once, quite unaccountably, he grew feverishly restless. He drained his glass and said: 'Come on, everybody, let's whip into Norwich!' Van Mentz looked up at the bar clock and shook his head. 'Not worth it. We'd never get there before closing time.' The others murmured in agreement. Tuck, Joyce and his bloodhound Shuffles jumped into his car and sped off. At the next crossroads he turned off for Coltishall (see *Fly For Your Life* by Larry Forrester, Frederick Muller Ltd, 1956). Did Tuck have a premonition of disaster? Throughout the war 'Tuck's Luck' served him to an almost supernatural degree. He was promoted to Wing Commander on 4 July 1941 and his place as 257 Squadron commander was taken by Squadron Leader 'Cowboy' Blatchford. Tuck died on 5 May 1987. (*See also Neatishead*)

Horsham St Faith and City of Norwich Aviation Museum (CONAM).

Description: RAF airfield 1939–43 and after the war, and used by the 8th Air Force 1942, 1943 and 1944–5. Now Norwich International Airport.

Location: On the A140 northbound Norwich – Cromer road.

142

The CONAM is on the northern edge of the airport.

Directions: Follow the road signs to Norwich Airport from the city centre and ring road. For the CONAM turn right after the main entrance.

Comments: Many of the wartime buildings and three of the original hangars remain because the airfield is now Norwich Airport and also an industrial complex. The former barracks and officers' mess buildings off Fifers Lane, which were used for a time as accommodation for students attending the University of East Anglia, have now been demolished to make way for housing. The former RAF married quarters and the officer housing in Fifers Lane are now private residences. A memorial dedicated to all units that flew from the airfield in the Second World War is situated next to the terminal building. (See also 2nd Air Division USAAF Memorial Library, Norwich.)

No trip to the region's airfields and tourist attractions is complete wtihout rounding everything off or starting with a visit to the museum, which was conceived and is run by a dedicated band of volunteers. A Vulcan bomber dominates the collection and a variety of other aircraft, both civilian and military, are also on display. Within the exhibition building are displays showing the development of aviation in Norfolk. An excellent gift shop sells books, models and other items. Opening Times: April to October: Tuesday to Saturday 10.00-5.00. Sunday and Bank Holidays 1200-5.00. School Holidays, 1200-5.00. November to March: Wednesday and Saturday 10.00-4.00. Sunday and Bank Holidays 12.00-4.00. Closed over Christmas and New Year. Admission prices vary. Children under 5 free. (Tel. 01603 893080).

RAF Units	From/To	Aircraft
110 Sqn det	June 1939?	Blenheim IV
21 Sqn det	November–December 1939	Blenheim IV
66 Sqn	16-29 May 1940	Spitfire I
19 Sqn	17 April–16 May 1940	Spitfire I
264 Sqn	May–July 1940	Defiant I
114 Sqn	10 June–August 1940	Blenheim IV
139 Sqn	10 June 1940–13 July 1941	Blenheim IV

1508 Flt	4 April–20 December 1941	Blenheim IV/Wellington
18 Sqn	13 July–5 November 1941	Blenheim IV
139 Sqn	23 October–9 December 1941	Mosquito B.IV
105 Sqn	9 Dec 1941–22 Sept 1942	Mosquito B.IV
18 Sqn	5 Dec 1941–4 March 1942	Blenheim IV
FTF	December 1941–21 Jan 1942	Hudson
1508 Flt	19 January 1942–14 April 1943	Oxford
139 Sqn	8 June–29 September 1942	Mosquito B.IV
MCU	30 August–29 September 1942	Mosquito
1655 MTU	30 August–28 September 1942	Blenheim/Mosquito
1444 Flt	U/K	Hudson
1689 Flt	15 February 1944–7 May 1945	Spitfire/Hurricane

Langham

Description: Originally a satellite of Bircham Newton and subsequently an independent station.

Location: On the B1388 between Binham and Langham villages.

Comments: Turkey-rearing sheds were built on the concrete areas, except for the north-east–south-west runway. Other unused sections of concrete were broken up in 1985 for road construction. The control tower and rare dome-trainer that at various times was used for anti-shipping and as an astro trainer for night navigation are amongst the buildings that survive. In 1999 The dome trainer was cosmetically restored. From the 1960s light civil aircraft have visited the airfield. In recent years a small blister-type hangar has been built and Mr Henry Labouchere runs an aircraft maintenance facility here. There is no memorial but inside the church are two plaques. One reads, 'To the Glory of God and in grateful remembrance of generous hospitality bestowed on the Netherlands sailors, soldiers and airmen during their stay in the United Kingdom *Annus Domini* 1940–1947. This tablet was presented by the Protestant Churches of the Netherlands. I was a stranger and ye took me in'. Another reads, 'From the fields between this church and the sea, during the wartime summer of 1944, a small band of young men flew in defence of these islands. Most of these ardent volunteers had journeyed half across the globe to our aid in a time of desperate need. The many successful attacks on enemy shipping made by pilots of 455 Sqn RAAF and 489 Sqn.RNZAF and their British navigators made a valuable contribution to the preservation of our freedom. Sadly many of these young men were destined never to return home again but to be lost somewhere across a waste of seas with their final resting place remaining unknown to this day. May their sacrifices for us be never forgotten'. Many of the hassocks are beautifully embroidered with the RAF badge and crests of squadrons stationed at Langham in the Second World War. Inside the church is a framed colour photograph of the hassocks.

RAF Units	From/To	Aircraft
1 AACU (K/M)det	July 1940–1 November 1942	Demon/Henley/Defiant TIII
280 Sqn	31 July–1 November 1942	Anson
819 Sqn FAA	July–August 1942	Swordfish
1611 Flt	1 Nov 1942–9 Nov 1942	Henley TT.III
1612 Flt	1 Nov 1942–8 Dec 1942	Henley T.III
2 AAPC	16 Feb 1943–17 June 1943	Lysander
1626 Flt	17 June 1943–30 Nov 1943	Lysander
280 Sqn	6 Sep–30 October 1944	Warwick ASR.I
455 Sqn	13 April–24 October 1944	Beaufighter TX.X
489 Sqn	8 April–24 October 1944	Beaufighter TF.X
521 Sqn	30 Oct 1944–3 Nov 1945	Gladiator II/Hudson III/V/Hurricane IIc/Spitfire IX
827 Sqn FAA	November–December 1944	Barracuda II
524 Sqn	1 November 1944–25 May 1945	Wellington GR.XIII
612 Sqn	17 Dec 1944–9 July 1945	Wellington GR.XIV
407 Sqn det	14 April–10 May 1945	Wellington GR.XIV
254 Sqn	26 Nov 1945–6 May 1946	Beaufighter/Mosquito
280 Sqn	3-23 November 1945	

Little Snoring

Description: 3 Group night bomber and 100 Group night intruder airfield in the Second World War.

Location: North of the A148 Fakenham – Holt Road and east of the Little Snoring – Great Snoring road.

Directions: Take the A1067 Norwich – Fakenham Road, branching off right just after the turn to Great Ryburgh. This avoids having to skirt Fakenham and will bring you out on the busy A148 Fakenham – Holt Road. Turn right and take the second turning to Little Snoring. The airfield is off to your right.

Comments: The airfield is still in use and the control tower situated in the middle remains in a relatively intact condition. In St Andrew's church nearby the 23 and 515 Squadron victory boards are to be found. The village sign in The Street at Snoring includes a propeller and Mosquito aircraft. Almost opposite the sign is the White House guest house run by Bryan and Celia Lee (01328 878789) which is an ideal location to break your journey. Many ex-100 Group veterans and their families stay here.

Units	From/To	Aircraft
115 Sqn	6 August–26 November 1943	Lancaster II
1678 HCU	6 August 1943–16 Sep 1943	Lancaster II
169 Sqn	8 December 1943–4 June 1944	Beaufighter VI/ Mosquito II
1692 Flt	10 Dec 1943–21 May 1944	Defiant I/Beaufighter II/ Anson I; Oxford II/ Mosquito FBVI
515 Sqn	12 Dec 1943–10 June 1945	Blenheim V/ Beaufighter If/ Mosquito II/FBVI
USAAF Intruder Det	March–April 1944	P-51 Mustang/ P-38 Lightning
23 Sqn	2 June 1944–25 Sep 1945	Mosquito FBVI/ NFXXX
141 Sqn	3 July 1945–7 Sep 1945	Mosquito NFXXX
1473 Flt	28 Nov 1943–12 Decr 1943	
2 CAACU	20 July 1951–23 March 1953	Spitfire XVI/ Mosquito TT35/ Vampire FBV

Ludham

Description: Satellite airfield for RAF Coltishall.

Location: About 13 miles north-east of Norwich and close to Hickling Broad.

Directions: Follow the A47 Norwich – Dereham road to Weston Longville.

Comments: The watch office, which is in good condition, is now a Grade II listed building and has been purchased by a KLM airline pilot, whose intention is to turn it into a holiday home.

Units	From/To	Aircraft
19 Sqn	1 Dec 1941–4 April 1942	Spitfire Vb
610 Sqn	4 April 1942–15 October 1942	Spitfire Vb/Vc
1489 Flt det	December 1942–1943	Lysander/Martinet
167 Sqn	14 Oct 1942–1 March 1943	Spitfire Vb/Vc
167 Sqn	15 March–13 May 1943	Spitfire Vb/Vc
195 Sqn	13 May 1943–31 Jul 1943	Typhoon Ib
611 Sqn	31 July 1943–4 Aug 1943	Spitfire Vb
602 Sqn	23 February–5 April 1945	Spitfire XVIe
603 Sqn	24 February–5 April 1945	Spitfire XVIe
91 Sqn	8 April 1945–14 Jul 1945	Spitfire 21
1 Sqn	14 May 1945–23 Jul 1945	Spitfire 21

Marham

Description: 2 Group bomber airfield in the Second World War.

Location: By the A1122 10 miles east of Downham Market and 9 miles south-east of King's Lynn.

Comments: After the war the station has been in continual use as a bomber airfield, the current incumbents being Tornadoes of Strike Command. The village sign near Holy Trinity Church was given to the parish by RAF Marham to mark the silver jubilee of the RAF; one of the four side panels shows an aeroplane of the Great War flying over Marham. Over 100 airmen, from the First

World War to the present are buried in Holy Trinity churchyard and war graves plot. Sixty-eight airmen are buried at Marham: Fourteen RCAF, eight RNZAF, three RAAF, five *Luftwaffe* and thirty-eight RAF of which twenty-six were members of 218 Squadron. Two of the dead were crew members of Wellington Ic R1470 of 115 Squadron which was shot down over the Wash by a Ju. 88 intruder of I/NJG2 flown by *Leutnant* Heinz Volker on 4 April 1941. Ten others were killed in the crash of Wellington III X3394 of 115 Squadron at Carol House Farm, near Swaffham, on 11 November 1941 while on a cross-country exercise and fuel consumption test when the starboard engine cut. Buried in All Saints churchyard in Narborough are fifteen airmen of the Great War. In King's Lynn several airmen and civilians with aviation connections are buried in Hardwick or Gayton Road cemeteries. The largest memorial is the mass grave of five airmen from 115 Squadron at Marham killed when the Angel Hotel in Norfolk Street was hit by one of four bombs dropped by a Do 217 on 12 June 1942. In all forty-two people died in the air raid.

Units	From/To	Aircraft
38 Sqn	5 May 1937–12 Nov 1940	Hendon/Wellington I
115 Sqn	15 June 1937–24 Sept 1942	Hendon/Wellington I
1 RNZAF Unit	1 June–27 Sep 1939	Wellington I
218 Sqn	December 1940–7 July 1942	Wellington/Stirling
3 Gp TTF	14 February 1940–18 November 1941	
105 Sqn	22 Sep 1942–23 March 1944	Mosquito IV
1418 Flt	December 1941–1 March 1942	Wellington
1483 (Bomber)	July 1942–29 June 1943	Wellington Ic & III/ Defiant I &II
Gunnery Training Flight		
ABTF	13 July 1942–15 Mar 1943	
1483 Flt	13 July 1942–29 June 1943	Lysander/Wellington
1427 Flt	4 August–2 October 1942	Stirling/Halifax
139 Sqn	29 Sep 1942–4 July 1943	Mosquito IV
109 Sqn	5 July 1943–2 April 1944	Mosquito IV/IX
1655 MTU	28 Sep 1942–1 May 1943	Mosquito IV
1655 MTU	July 1943–7 March 1944	Mosquito IV

Matlaske

Description: Satellite airfield for RAF Coltishall.

Location: 5 miles from Holt and 12 miles north-west of Coltishall.

Comments: Abandoned by the RAF in 1945, it was briefly used as a PoW camp before the airfield was returned to agriculture. Today very little except the perimeter track remains of the Second World War airfield.

Units	From/To	Aircraft
72 Sqn	30 October–2 November 1940	Spitfire I
601 Sqn	2 July–16 August 1941	Hurricane II/Airacobra I
ASR Flt	July–1 October 1941	Walrus
19 Sqn	16 August–1 December 1941	Spitfire
222 Sqn	6 June–1 July 1941	Spitfire II/Vb
278 Sqn	1 October 1941–10 April 1942	Lysander I/Walrus
12 Gp TTF	13 April–8 December 1942	Lysander I
137 Sqn	1 Dec 1941–24 August 1942	Whirlwind I
266 Sqn	2-11 August 1942	Typhoon Ib
56 Sqn	24 August 1942–22 July 1943	Typhoon I
1489 Flt	13 April–2 June 1943	Lysander TT.III/Martinet
19 Sqn	4–20 June 1943	Mustang III
609 Sqn	22 July–18 August 1943	Typhoon Ia/Ib
611 Sqn	1–31 July 1943	Spitfire IX
195 Sqn	31 July–21 August 1943	Typhoon Ib
56 Sqn	23–28 September 1944	Tempest V
3 Sqn	21–28 September 1944	Tempest V
122 Sqn	28 September–14 October 1944	Mustang III
19 Sqn	28 September–4 October 1944	Mustang III
65 Sqn	29 September–14 October 1944	Mustang III
229 Sqn	22 October–20 November 1944	Mustang III
486 Sqn	9–28 September 1944	Tempest V
602 Sqn	18 October–20 November 1944	Spitfire IX

451 Sqn	23 February–6 April 1945	Spitfire XVI
453 Sqn RAAF	18 October 1944–6 April 1945	Spitfire IX/XVI
658 Sqn	10 July–2 October 1945	Auster
659 Sqn	10 July–2 October 1945	Auster

Neatishead

Description: Formerly an RAF radar station now the Air Defence Museum, which is housed in the original operations building.

Location: On the A1062 Coltishall – Ludham road opposite the turn for Horning.

Directions: Take the A1151 from Norwich to Wroxham where a turn right is made onto the A1062.

Comments: The end of the Cold War means that the hitherto secret world of air defence is now open to all. The Air Defence Museum opened in October 1994 and is a registered charity. It traces the history and development of the air defence of the UK during the period 1935–1990. This includes command and control of ground-stationed and airborne radar systems, Second World War operations at home and overseas, surface-to-air missiles, radar engineering development, ground-to-ground and ground-to-air communications systems, the development of aircraft detection from sound to modern radar systems and aerial photography. Current features include, Battle of Britain operations and control exhibits of 1940, an accurate recreation of a 1942 GCI operations room, the original 'Cold War' ops room used until 1993, a Second World War ROC field post, including associated equipment, the largest permanent display of original unit and station badges and ROC and air defence model aircraft collection originally housed in Bentley Priory. The village sign incorporates the badge of RAF Neatishead. (*See also Horning and Coltishall.*)

Opening Hours: 10.00 to 16.00 on the following days: Second Saturday of each month and each Bank Holiday Monday. Group Visits may be arranged outside these times, e.g. weekday evenings. Please contact: The Museum Manager, Air Defence Museum, RAF Neatishead, Norwich NR12 8YB.
Tel. 01692 633309.
http://.chide.museum.org.uk/

Oulton

Description: Light bomber, heavy bomber conversion and 100 Group RCM airfield in the Second World War.

Location: In the parish of Oulton Street to the east of the B1149 Norwich – Holt road.

Directions: Take the B1149 Norwich – Holt Road and the next turn right after the roundabout on the Cawston – Aylsham road (B1145). Be very careful after taking the right turn to Oulton Street when driving because nearing the end of the airfield runway (huts will be seen on your left) a semi-concealed hump in the road is liable to take your undercarriage off!

Comments: A few huts remain, the control tower having been demolished in December 1999 after being declared unsafe. On Sunday, 15 May 1994 the Bishop of Lynn formally dedicated a memorial to RAF Oulton built of red brick at the crossroads north of Oulton Street.

A total of fifty-six Bomber Command aircraft were lost flying in operations from Oulton: thirty-four Blenheims, two Bostons, a Ventura, sixteen Fortresses and three Liberators. The plaque of Cumbrian stone has the inscription, 'RAF Oulton 1940–45, in Grateful Tribute to those members of the British Commonwealth and American Air Forces who served at RAF Oulton and in honour of those that gave their lives. Those who died for our freedom will live forever in our hearts.' Below is a listing of all the squadrons and units stationed here. Also, a book of remembrance has been placed in St Andrew's church at Blickling. Combine your visit with a vist to Blickling Hall. The National Trust house and park with its lake will delight the whole family and the Buckinghamshire Arms has a bar and accommodation including four-poster beds! A walk around the lake and fishing is free.

On 18 July 1992 a brass memorial plaque was unveiled at the base of one of the radar towers of the wartime RAF Stoke Holy Cross, near Poringland, Norwich, fifty years after a Blenheim IV crashed into it killing all the crew. The plaque is inscribed, 'No. 18 Squadron, Royal Air Force, Blenheim aircraft Z7304 crashed into the pylons at this site, July 18th 1942. Crew: Pilot Officer Henry Lowter RAFVR, Sgt Gerard Crawford RAF, Sgt Kenneth Custance Ellis RAF and Kenneth Thomas Tagg Esq. Meteorologist.'

On 11 February 1938 Bristol Blenheim K7199 of 144 Squadron from RAF Hemswell, Lincs, crashed during a heavy storm at Oulton Hall and the three crew were killed. In 1995 a memorial was re-erected in the grounds of Oulton Hall in the form of a tree, marked by a plaque. Blenheim IV 12279 of 114 Squadron crashed into woods at Heydon following engine failure on take-off on 4 December 1940. This was the first of four crashes of Oulton-based Blenheims in the area during the early years of hostilities. (*See also Blickling Hall.*)

Units	From/To	Aircraft
114 Sqn	10 August 1940–2 March 1941	Blenheim IV
18 Sqn	3 April–13 July 1941	Blenheim IV
139 Sqn	13 July 1941–23 October 1941	Blenheim IV
18 Sqn	November–December 1941	Blenheim IV
139 Sqn	Dec 1941/15–20 June 1942	Hudson III
236 Sqn	3 July–19 September 1942	Beaufighter Ic
21 Sqn	1 April–27 Sep 1943	Ventura I/II
88 Sqn	29 Sept 1942–30 March 1943	Boston III/IIIa
1699 Flight	May–June 1944	Fortress I/II/III/ Liberator VI
803rd BS/36th BG USAAF	May-August 1944	B-17F/G/B-24H/ J/M Liberator
214 Squadron	23 May 1944–29 July 1945	Fortress IIa/III
223 Squadron	23 August 1944–29 July 1945	Fortress II/III/ Liberator VI
274 MU	Nov 1945–Nov 1946	Mosquito (storage)

Scottow

Comment: Buried in RAF Coltishall's cemetery at Scottow are fifty-five airmen who lost their lives in the Second World War: twenty-four RAF, fifteen RCAF, three RNZAF and eight *Luftwaffe*. Of these, seven were airmen of 68 Squadron, including six Czechs. Four of six airmen killed in the crash of Wellington X1695 are buried here. The aircraft of 23 OTU at Pershore fell on marshes 1 mile south of the Stracey Arms public house on 26 January 1943. There are graves of five airmen of 255 Squadron

Buried in the RAF cemetery at Scottow are fifty-five airmen who lost their lives in the Second World War. They include twenty-four RAF, eight *Luftwaffe* and seven airmen of 68 Squadron, including six who were Czechs. (*Author*)

killed flying Beaufighters and a Blenheim. Five graves are of Spitfire pilots of 19, 222, 610 and 616 Squadrons. Other airmen include Sergeant Vaclav Brejcha of 257 Squadron killed on 19 June 1941 when the Station Flight Tiger Moth crashed near Lowestoft. Pilot Officer N. N. Campbell, a pilot of 242 Squadron, died on 17 October 1940 when a Do 17 shot down Hurricane V6575 in the sea. Also buried here is an American civilian, Mr Otto W. Kanturek (forty-two) of 20th Century Fox Films Ltd, who was killed on 26 June 1941 when filming a 257 Squadron Hurricane from a 500 Squadron Anson for the film *A Yank in the RAF*. The two aircraft collided and the Hurricane pilot was the only survivor.

The *Luftwaffe* graves are of: *Feldwebel* Heinz Genähr (buried at Scottow, 11 June 1941) of Do 17Z 4248/US+DA of Stab/KG2, which was shot down by Flying Officer J. R. D. 'Bob' Braham DFC and Sergeant Ross of 29 Squadron in a Beaufighter If during a raid on Hull on 14 March 1941 and crashed into the sea southeast of Skegness Pier at 2145 hours; *Obergefreiter* Herbert Sehnert, *Bordfunker* (radio operator) (buried at Scottow 11 June 1941) of Heinkel He 111H-5, 7045/A1+DP of 6KG/53, which was shot down during an attack on Sheffield on 9 May 1941; *Feldwebel* Oskar Haug; *Unteroffizier* Richard Proska; *Feldwebel* Hans Trokes; who (buried at Scottow 5 March 1942) were killed when Ju 88A-4, 1384/4D+DA of Erpro/KG30 was hit by anti-aircraft fire near Mundesley at 1620 hours on 4 March 1942; *Unteroffizier* Erich Ohnesorge, who was killed on 29 July 1942 when Do 217E-4 1213/US+DP of 6/KG2 was shot down by a Beaufighter of 68 Squadron flown by Flying Officer Raybould and Flight Sergeant Mullaley and crashed on Salthouse Marshes, Sheringham; *Leutnant* Wolfgang Louth, who was killed when Flight Lieutenant W. D. Winard and Pilot Officer C. K. Wood of 68 Squadron in a Beaufighter shot down Ju 88D-l 1342/8H+KL of 3 (F)/33 on 19 October 1942, the Junkers crashed in the sea 20 miles north of Cromer and Louth's body was washed ashore at Cromer on 17 November 1942 and interred at Scottow cemetery that day; and *Ein Deutscher Soldaten*, possibly that of August Fellemann of KG30. A Ju 88 of that unit was shot down at sea with only one survivor. The pilot, *Leutnant* Stepulat, was posthumously awarded the *Ritterkreuz*. The third member of the crew, August Fellmann, was not accounted for. However, an unidentified body of a German airman was washed ashore at Trimingham some months later.

Over twenty-five airmen have been buried in the war graves plot since the war, including Flying Officer Peter Watson, who

The *Luftwaffe* graves of *Obergefreiter* Herbert Sehnert of 6KG/53, who was killed during an attack on Sheffield on 9 May 1941 and *Feldwebel* Heinz Genähr of Stab/KG2, who was killed on 14 March 1941. (*Author*)

was flying a Mosquito on a night interception exercise on 25 May 1948 when it collided with a Proctor over Saxlingham, Norfolk. The Proctor returned safely but the Mosquito crashed, killing the crew. The navigator, Flying Officer Marsh, was due for demob in a week's time. Flight Lieutenant A Gavin (forty-seven) and Master Navigator H. W. E. Crossman (forty-three) were two of three airmen killed on 22 June 1967 when their ASR Whirlwind (XJ414 of 202 Squadron) crashed into the sea off Caister-on-Sea Golf Club. Flight Lieutenant Greg Noble, a Jaguar pilot on 41 Squadron, who was killed taking off from Coltishall on 23 January 1996, was laid to rest in the cemetery within yards of where he died.

Sculthorpe

Description: Light bomber, and RCM training airfield for 100 Group in the Second World War.

Location: Between the village of the same name and Syderstone to the west, north of the A148 Fakenham – King's Lynn road.

Directions: Follow the A148 Fakenham bypass towards King's Lynn and turn right onto the A1067 Docking road.

Comments: Extremely difficult to view as the air base is part of STANTA and is used by MoD and USAAF units, mainly by Army Air Corps and RAF units on exercise in the region. The former technical area is now the Tattersett Business Park and businesses occupy many of the buildings such as the 796 Medical Aid Station.

Units	From/To	Aircraft
342 Lorraine Sqn	15 May–19 July 1943	Boston IIIa
21 Sqn	27 Sept–31 Dec 1943	Mosquito FBVI
464 Sqn RAAF	21 July–31 December 1943	Ventura I/II/ Mosquito FBVI
487 Sqn RNZAF	20 July–31 December 1943	Ventura I/II/ Mosquito FBVI
MCF	22 August 1943?	
214 Squadron	16 January–16 May 1944	Stirling/Fortress II
803rd BS USAAF	March–May 1944	B-17F/G
1699 Flt	24 April–16 May 1944	Fortress

Stratton Strawless Hall

Description: Operations room for RAF Coltishall.

Location: North on the A140 Norwich – Aylsham road.

Comments: Early in 1940 Squadron Leader Bader took the stage at the Odeon Cinema in Norwich to promote recruitment of WAAF personnel to work in the operations room at Coltishall. (In *Reach For The Sky,* Paul Brickhill says, 'Bader fell noisily often but always rose and "pressed on". At a cinema in Norwich he tripped in the aisle one night and dented his right kneecap so that the leg hung crookedly. He merely dragged himself to the nearest seat, called an usherette to bring him a screwdriver from the projection room, pulled up his trouser leg, made a few adjustments and was mobile again.') Those who volunteered were summoned to Coltishall, uniformed and taken straight to the operations room with no training for the task or for RAF life in general. The operations room was soon closed and relocated to a single-story wooden hut at Catton near Norwich with the duty watch being transported from Coltishall on a daily basis. Catton proved unsuitable and Norwich was being bombed regularly by the *Luftwaffe* so the operations room relocated to remote Stratton Strawless Hall, where a purpose designed operations room was built adjacent to the original buildings. Nissen huts were also constructed in the grounds to house RAF and WAAF personnel. For those lucky enough to be billeted in the hall, or

Stratton Strawless Hall in 2006. (*Author*)

'Gin Palace', as it was popularly known, it was an escape from the inevitable discipline of life at Coltishall. One of the WAAFs was Corporal Bunty Walmsley, who signed on in 1940. She remembers that sunbathing on the roof of the hall was a favourite off-duty or between-shifts pastime. This activity was terminated when American pilots began making a beeline for the hall to admire the view! One day in 1940 Bunty and other members of her watch were abruptly aroused from their beds and told to assemble immediately outside to be addressed by the WAAF CO. Garbed in various forms of night attire, they all staggered outside looking the worst for wear The next moment their CO appeared dressed in full uniform and informed them that the Germans had invaded the south coast and that further landings were likely. If Coltishall should he involved, she expected each and every one of them to defend the station in the best possible way. Bunty decided that her only weapon was a poker allocated to her billet! (*See also Coltishall.*)

Swanton Morley

Description: Light bomber, day bomber and 100 Group support airfield in the Second World War.

Location: 2 miles north-north-east of East Dereham.

Directions: Follow the A47 Norwich – King's Lynn road and turn off where the sign says Swanton Morley Windmill. Head on through the village and turn left towards the old airfield, although unless you are in the army or have prior permission, entry is out of the question. (On the Worthing side of the airfield is the T2 hangar previously used by the Mosquito Flight which can be reached by following the road through the village and turning sharp left before the church and along a rough winding road past a pill box.)

Comments: This RAF station closed in 1996 when the airfield was taken over by the British Army for Robertson Barracks, home of the Light Dragoons. The J and T2 hangars were demolished for new AFV buildings but the rare watch office with meteorological section designed in 1939 was saved and in December 2005 it became a Grade II listed building. <u>Do not</u>

forget to look for the haunted former services' cinema!

Thirteen Second World War airmen of the RAF, RCAF and RNZAF are buried in All Saints churchyard. There are also eight post-war graves, including that of Corporal Hugh Jonathon Spencer (seventeen), Radley College Cadet Force, who was killed in the crash of Cadet TX3 glider XE804 of 614 Gliding School at Swanton Morley. The church has a stained glass window subscribed by RAF Swanton Morley.

In 1941 the directors and staff of Norwich Union raised £5,000 to buy a Spitfire for the RAF. Their presentation aircraft was Spitfire IIa P8140, built at Castle Bromwich and named *NUFLIER*. Inside the Norwich Union Museum in Surrey Street is a plaque inscribed, 'In the hour of peril, Norwich Union Insurance Society earned the gratitude of the British Nations sustaining the valour of the Royal Air Force and fortifying the cause of freedom by the gift of a Spitfire aircraft. They shall mount up with wings as eagles. Issued by the Ministry of Aircraft Production, 1941.' The City regalia in City Hall includes a solid silver model of a Boulton Paul Overstrand presented to the City by Boulton and Paul Ltd in 1958 to commemorate the fortieth anniversary of the RAF.

Units	From/To	Aircraft
105 Sqn	31 October 1940–8 December 1941	Blenheim
88 Sqn	8 July–1 August 1941	Blenheim
152 Sqn	31 August–1 December 1941	Spitfire
1515 Flt	22 Sep 1941–1 November 1943	Oxford
226 Sqn	9 Dec 1941–13 Feby 1944	Boston IIIa/Mitchell
15th BS USAAF	June 1942–July 1942	Boston
88 Sqn	30 March–19 August 1943	Boston III
1508 Flt	29 August 1943–24 June 1944	Oxford
305 (Polish) Sqn	5 Sep–18 November 1943	Wellington/Mitchell
1482 Flt	1 December 1943–1 April 1944	Mitchell/Martinet
3 Sqn	28 Dec 1943–14 Feb 1944	Typhoon
464 RAAF Sqn	25 March–8 April 1944	Mosquito
98 Sqn	March–10 April 1944	Mitchell
2 GSU	1 April 1944–1 August 1945	Boston/Anson/Martinet

180 Sqn	2–26 April 1944	Mitchell III
613 Sqn	11–24 April 1944	Mosquito FBVI
487 Sqn RNZAF	25–30 April 1944	Mosquito FBVI
100 Gp CF	December 1944–June 1945	
BSDU	December 1944–July 1945	various

Watton

Description: RAF light bomber station until August 1942, when it was allocated to the USAAF.

Location: East of Watton.

Directions: Off the B1108 Norwich – Watton road just before the town. Look for the huge decomissioned radio mast.

Comments: The 250 acre airfield was built in 1938–9 for the RAF, which operated Blenheims and other aircraft from the station until August 1942 when it was reallocated to the USAAF. The Americans took over Watton completely on 4 October 1943. Now part of STANTA, the main airfield site is off limits but many ex-wartime buildings such as the NAAFI and accommodation blocks on the opposite side of the Norwich–Watton road have been modified for industrial and commercial use. The buildings, including the guardhouse and hangars and family quarters on the airfield site, are relatively intact. Near the side of the now demolished officers' mess is a memorial erected in May 1990 containing a twisted Blenheim propeller and two plaques, inscribed: 'To the memory of those of the Royal Air Force and Commonwealth Air Forces who lost their lives while serving at Watton and Bodney,' and 'This propeller was recovered from Blenheim R3800 which was shot down at Aalborg, Denmark, on 13 August 1940 whilst operating out of Watton.' A third plaque commemorates the 8th Air Force units that served at Watton. And in the grounds of Griston village church there is a memorial to the 3rd Strategic Air Depot.

Units	From/To	Aircraft
34 Sqn	2 March–12 August 1939	Blenheim I
21 Sqn	2 March 1939–24 June 1940	Blenheim I/IV

82 Sqn	25 August 1939–21 March 1942	Blenheim I/IV
18 Sqn	20–26 May 1940	Blenheim IV
105 Sqn	10 Jul 1940–31 October 1940	Blenheim IV
90 Sqn	7–15 May 1941	Fortress I
21 Sqn	14 June–26 December 1941	Blenheim IV
1508 Flt	20 December 1941–19 Jan 1942	Oxford II
17 (P) AFU	29 Jan 1942–1 May 1943	Master II
803rd RG	22 April–9 August 1944	B-17/B-24
25th BG (R) USSAF	9 August 1944–23 July 1945	B-17/B-24/A-26/P-38/L-5

Weasenham Hall

Description: Part of the house was used as an officers' mess for RAF West Raynham and Great Massingham.

Location: About 2 miles from West Raynham airfield.

Comments: In the Second World War Weasenham Hall (now demolished) belonged to Major the Hon. Richard Coke, fifth son to the second Earl of Leicester and his French wife Elizabeth, known affectionately as 'Pheas'. At the end of 1940 part of the house was requisitoned to serve as an RAF officers' mess following a need to disperse after enemy tip-and-run raids between May and October on West Raynham and Massingham had caused some damage and deaths. On 19 July a raider dropped twenty-one bombs on RAF West Raynham causing a fire in a hangar, which destroyed part of the roof and burned out three Ansons and damaged other aircraft. On 27 October an enemy aircraft dropped incendiaries causing the first deaths to enemy action. Weasenham Hall also proved a useful venue for VIP visitors to Great Massingham and West Raynham such as Prince Bernhardt of the Netherlands on 27 October 1941 after he had inspected the Drem lighting system at the airfield. The 'Groupe Lorraine' Squadron, 342, were lucky to be billeted for a time at the house where Mrs Coke, herself French, made them feel very much at home. This was about the time that the 'Cafe de Paris' was bombed and this establishment had a 'very good band and better chefs'. The chefs were sent to West Raynham in RAF uniform and Mrs. Coke recalled:

> *The English didn't know much about the Cafe de Paris but only that the frogs couldn't talk properly so they made them wash cars. The poor French squadron watched the cooks washing cars and ate the most awful food cooked by people who couldn't cook – pain and grief to them! The band used to play on rum and lime and when they finished playing at West Raynham they would board a truck and come to Weasenham Hall where the playing continued until the steward would pull back the curtains and announce 'Breakfast is served!'*

Long after they left the hall the aircrew kept in touch and letters and cards poured in from the Middle East, North Africa, Sicily, Italy and of course some PoW camps, as well as from other RAF stations. Later in the war the house became a mobile field hospital for the RAF and on occasion agents from the Special

Weasenham Hall, now demolished, close by the A1065 Swaffham–Fakenham road photographed in November 2005. In the Second World War the property belonged to the Coke family and at the end of 1940 part of the house was requisitoned to serve as an RAF officers' mess following enemy raids on RAF West Raynham and the satellite at Great Massingham, which caused some deaths and damage. (*Author*)

Operations Executive would arrive for a brief rest between flights to occupied Europe.

In 1943 Flight Sergeant Mike Henry, a 107 Squadron Boston air gunner was billeted at Weasenham Hall and went to Great Massingham by bus.

> We were plagued with plover and in order to try and scare them off we begged, borrowed and obtained as many shotguns as possible and walked line abreast across the grass airfield. The birds got up long before we were in range and as soon as we returned so did the plover. We then decided to drive across in a variety of vehicles – from the station ambulance to a fire tender, flight vans etc – guns poking out of windows and from the tops of some vehicles. We did manage to close with the birds (they didn't seem frightened of vehicles) and we bagged quite a number. However, they still remained a menace ... We often held clay pigeon shoots during our stand-by hours. I was a reasonably good shot and with sixpences in the kitty for the winner I wound up tying with another gunner. He won (he was a former gamekeeper).

West Raynham

Description: Day light bomber, night intruder and 100 Group night intruder airfield in the Second World War.

Location: 5 miles south-west of Fakenham and 2 miles west of West Raynham village.

Directions: Take the A1067 Norwich – Fakenham road and branch off left along the B1145 to a point where it meets the A1065. Turn right and follow the signs for West Raynham (not forgetting to see Great Massigham during the journey).

Comments: Although off limits and protected by MoD security there is much to see, including the Station HQ, chapel, airmen's restaurant (with upstairs cinema) and hangars etc., as the station remains relatively intact although in a state of disrepair following its closure in 1994.

A memorial to Pilot Officer John Graham's crew of a 114 Squadron Blenheim that crashed at Brisley village pond near Dereham returning from Essen in 18 June 1942 killing all three crew has been erected (www.acess-web.com/users/mconstab /blenheim). Nine airmen are buried in Fakenham's Queen's Road Cemetery including men of 18, 107 and 114 Blenheim squadrons and Count Gabriel Antoine Armand de Gramont, who on 10 April 1943 was killed on a training flight in a Boston of 342 Lorraine Squadron at West Raynham. His inspirational epitaph, 'Happy are those who are hungry and thirsty for justice because they will be satisfied'. pays tribute to the young French aristocrat described as a mixture of Joan of Arc and Don Quixote. As the eldest son of the Duc de Gramont, he spent his youth in Paris and at the family castle at Valliere before joining the army. It was while working as a diplomat in Washington that he became concerned about the growth of Hitler's power and returned to France to join the French air force in 1939. He immediately responded to the broadcast by General de Gaulle on 18 June 1940 calling for French nationals to fight Nazism and fled France from Biarritz in a small fishing boat after sending his wife Marie Helene and three sons back to Washington. He joined the Free French and trained as a bomber pilot in South Africa before being posted to England in January 1943, where he took part in bombing operations but three months later the 34-year-old was killed when his Boston crashed on approach to West Raynham after running out of fuel during a training flight in thick fog.

Units	From/To	Aircraft
101 Sqn	6 May 1939–1 Jul 1941	Blenheim IV/ Wellington Ic
90 Sqn	10 May–7 Sep 1939	Blenheim I/IV
2 Gp Pool	14–19 Sep 1939	
2 Gp TTF	October 1939–Mar 1941	Blenheim I/Battle II/ Lysander II/Tutor
76 Sqn	30 April–20 May 1940	Hampden I
139 Sqn	30 May–10 June 1940	Blenheim IV
18 Sqn	8 Sep 1940–3 April 1941	Blenheim 1V
90 Sqn	14 May–28 June 1941	Blenheim IV
268 Sqn	20–21 June 1941	Tomahawk
114 Sqn	19 July 1941–15 Nov 1942	Blenheim IV/V
1420 Flt	19 July 1941–15 Nov 1941	Blenheim IV
2 Gp TTF	30 September–November 1941	Lysander

1482 Flt	November 1941–29 May 1943	Lysander/Blenheim/Defiant
98 Sqn	12 Sep–15 October 1942	Mitchell
180 Sqn	13 Sep–19 October 1942	Mitchell
342 Sqn	7 April–15 May 1943	Boston
1482 Flt	17 Sept–1 December 1943	Mitchell/Martinet
141 Sqn	4 December 1943–3 July 1945	Beaufighter/Mosquito II/FBVI/NFXXX
239 Sqn	9 December 1943–1 Jul 1945	Mosquito II/FBVI/NFXXX
1694 Flt	24 Jan–21 May 1944	Martinet
BSDU	10 April–May 1944	Mosquito FBVI/NFXIX

Weybourne

Description: Anti-aircraft gunnery practice camp.

Location: off the A149 3 miles west of Sheringham.

Directions: Follow the signs from near Bodham on A148 or from village centre on the A149.

Comments: Combine your visit with a trip to the Muckleburgh Collection, Weybourne, Holt, NR25 7EG, Norfolk's largest working military museum (www.muckleburgh.co.uk, 07747 798393), and also the Poppy Line, otherwise known as the North Norfolk Railway, with stations at Weybourne, Holt and Sheringham (NNR Plc, The Station, Sheringham NR26 8RA, www.nnr.co.uk 01263 820800. Talking timetable 01263 820808). Weybourne station is south east of the village.

Units	From/To	Aircraft
AACU	16 May 1939–?	Wallace/Henley/Beaufighter TT10/Mosquito TT35
		Queen Bee drones

ORDER OF BATTLE, 6 JUNE 1944, RAF BOMBER AND FIGHTER UNITS IN NORFOLK

Station	Unit	Aircraft Type
Bircham Newton	279 Squadron	Hudson III/V/VI
	415 Squadron (Det)	Wellington GR.XII
	695 Squadron	Henley TT.III/ Martinet TT-I/Hurricane
Coltishall	316 Squadron	Mustang III
	504 Squadron (B Flight)	Spitfire Vb
	25 Squadron	Mosquito NF.XVII
Docking	521 Squadron (Met)	Ventura V/Gladiator II/ Hurricane II
	2 APC	Martinet
	1525 BAT Flight	Oxford
Downham Market	635 Squadron	Lancaster I/III
Feltwell	3 LFS	Lancaster
	1519 BAT Flight	Oxford
Foulsham	BSDU	Mosquito FBVI/XIX
	192 Squadron	Wellington X/ Halifax III/Mosquito IV
Great Massingham	169 Squadron	Mosquito II/FBVI/XIX/ Beaufighter I/VI
	1692 (BS) Flight	Mosquito/Beaufighter
	1694 (TT) Flight	Martinet
Langham	455 and 489 Squadrons	Beaufighter X
Little Snoring	23 and 515 Squadrons	Mosquito FBVI

Matlaske	19 Squadron	Mustang III
	56 Squadron	Tempest V
North Creake	199 Squadron	Stirling III
Oulton	214 Squadron/1699 Flight	Fortress II/III
Swannington	85 Squadron	Mosquito IX
	157 Squadron	Mosquito XVII
Swanton Morley	2 Group Support Unit	Mitchell/Boston/Mosquito
	1508 BAT Flight	Oxford
West Raynham	141 Squadron/239 Squadron	Mosquito FBVI

BIBLIOGRAPHY AND FURTHER READING

Baldwin, Jim (editor), *RAF Sculthorpe: 50 Years of Watching & Waiting.* (Privately Published) 1999

Bartram, Len, *RAF Docking and Bircham Newton* (Privately published)

Bartram, Len, *RAF Foulsham 1942–54* (Privately published)

Bateman, John, *A War Record* (unpublished)

Boiten, Theo, *Blenheim Strike* (ARP) 1995

Boiten, Theo, *Bristol Blenheim* (Crowood Aviation Series) 1998

Bowman Martin W., *Low Level From Swanton* (ARP) 1995

Bowman, Martin W., *De Havilland Mosquito* (Crowood Aviation Series 1997)

Bowman Martin W., *Wellington: The Geodetic Giant* (Airlife) 1998

Bowman Martin W., *RAF Bomber Stories* (PSL) 1998

Bowman Martin W., *The Men Who Flew the Mosquito* (Pen & Sword Aviation) 2003

Bowman Martin W., *Mosquitopanik!* (Pen & Sword Aviation) 2004

Bowman Martin W., *Sentimental Journey* (Erskine Press) 2005

Bowman Martin W., *Echoes of East Anglia* (Halsgrove Publishing Ltd) 2006

Bowman, Martin W., *Mosquito Bomber/Fighter-Bomber Units 1942–45* (Osprey Combat Aircraft 4 1997)

Bowyer, Michael J. F., *2 Group RAF: A Complete History 1936–1945* (Faber & Faber) 1974

Bowyer, Michael J. F., *Action Stations 1: East Anglia* (PSL) 1990

Bowyer, Michael J. F., *Action Stations Revisited. No.1 Eastern England* (Crecy) 2000

Brickhill, Paul, *Reach For The Sky* (Collins) 1954

Butterworth, Arthur, *We Shall Be There: A History of 107 Squadron, 1918–1963* Air Britain 1990

Congdon, Philip, *Behind the Hangar Doors* (Sonik)

Fairhead, Huby & Tuffen, Roy, *Airfields and Airstrips of Norfolk and Suffolk* (Norfolk & Suffolk Aviation Museum)

Forrester, Larry, *Fly For Your Life* (Frederick Muller Ltd) 1956

Francis, Paul, *Military Airfield Architecture From Airships to the Jet Age* (PSL) 1996

Freeman, Roger A., *Bases of Bomber Command Then and Now* (After the Battle) 2001

Gunn, Peter B. *RAF Great Massingham: A Norfolk Airfield at War 1940–1946* (Privately Published) 1990

Henry DFC, Mike, *Air Gunner* (Goodall)

Innes, Graham Buchan, *British Airfield Buildings Expansion and Inter-War Periods* (Midland) 2000

Innes, Graham Buchan, *British Airfield Buildings of the Second World War* (Midland) 1995

Jefford, Wing Commander C. J., *RAF Squadrons* (Airlife) 1988

Jennings, Mick MBE, *RAF Coltishall Fighter Station; A Station History* (No.1 AIDU) 1998

Johnson, 'Johnnie' *Wing Leader* (Hamlyn) 1974

Kloos, Jan P, *320 Squadron RAF Memorial* 1940–1945 (1987)

Lambennont, Paul, *Lorraine Squadron* (Cassell) 1956

Lincoln, Paul, *The Aalborg Attack* (After the Battle No. 72)

Marriott, Leo, *British Military Airfields Then and Now* (Ian Allan Publishing) 1997

McKenzie, Roderick, *Ghost Fields of Norfolk* (Larks Press) 2004

Middlebrook, Martin and Chris Everitt, *The Bomber Command War Diaries: An Operational Reference Book 1939–1945* (Penguin) 1990

Moore, Jim, *Churchill's Light Cavalry* (2 vol) (unpublished)

Rijken, Kees and Paul Schepers *Operation Oyster* (unpublished)

Rønnest, Ole, *Aalborg 13 August 1940* (Privately published)

Scott, Stuart R., *Battle-Axe Blenheims: No. 105 Squadron RAF at War 1940–1* (Sutton) 1996

Scott, Stuart R., *Mosquito Thunder* (Sutton) 1999

Sharp, Martin and Bowyer Michael J. F., *Mosquito C* (Faber & Faber) 1967

Smith David J., *Britain's Memorials and Mementoes* (PSL) 1992

Smith, Graham, *Norfolk Airfields in the Second World War* (Countryside) 1994

Walker, Peter M., *Norfolk Military Airfields; An Operational Record 1913–1997* (Privately published) 1997